Executive Remuneration

by Geoffrey Newman.
F.T.I.I., F.C.I.I., A.C.I.S., A.I.Arb

READY REFERENCE SERIES

GUILD PRESS

READY REFERENCE SERIES

The Ready Reference Series comprises a sequence of books that provide a practical interpretation of the complicated legal, tax and accounting aspects of current legislation in those areas that are of vital importance to business.

The series aims to explain the issues in a concise and practical form enabling the reader to optimise a trading position or solve a legal or tax problem to his best advantage.

The Ready Reference Series is aimed at the professional advisor and the informed businessman. Base references to the sections of appropriate Acts are quoted in the text of the books to aid the professional advisor in producing a detailed brief on a particular problem.

Each book follows the same basic format with a detailed index, a summary of sources referred to, and, where appropriate, a glossary of terms, and an outline history leading up to the present legislation.

Any professional practice or business should derive considerable benefit from collecting the series. Books are updated as and when appropriate and purchasers are informed of the latest editions.

EXECUTIVE REMUNERATION by Geoffrey Newman

©*Copyright 1977 by Geoffrey Newman*

Published by
Guild Press, Park Place House, Tunnel Street, St. Helier, Jersey

Printed by Colour Artisans, Beccles, Suffolk

CONTENTS

PREFACE

In any text book, the author is faced with the dilemma of fitting as much relevant material as possible within the space allowed. Of necessity, some items, although interesting in themselves, have to be omitted because they are not of interest to readers generally.

Hopefully the information contained in this book will be useful to most readers but I am conscious of the fact that there is always room for improvement. I would therefore be grateful to receive suggestions from readers as to how future editions of the book may be improved.

Geoffrey G. Newman
65 Grosvenor Street
London W1X 9DB

CHAPTER 1

INTRODUCTION

The object of this book is to explain to companies, their professional advisers and their directors and employees the present fiscal system as it applies to all emoluments derived by people taxable under Schedule E. Schedule E deals with anyone who is regarded as "employed", and includes directors of companies in its scope.

The high rates of inflation experienced during recent years, coupled with pay restrictions and very high marginal tax rates, have meant that Schedule E taxpayers are generally more aware of their financial position and are increasingly anxious to improve it, if humanly and legally possible.

This book therefore attempts to provide an up-to-date analysis of Schedule E taxation as it stands at September 1977. The legislation affecting benefits in kind for directors and senior employees was fundamentally altered by the 1976 Finance Act, and the recent 1977 Finance Act has made important changes in areas such as overseas emoluments, overseas travelling and rent-free accommodation. However, quite apart from dealing with the purely legislative aspects, the book also attempts to outline current Inland Revenue practice in certain areas with which advisers and employers may not always be fully conversant.

The text begins with a general introduction to the problems of Schedule E and deals initially with the general taxation rules. It then goes on to consider the problems of directors and senior employees in the light of recent legislation, particularly in important areas such as company cars, pension schemes, overseas emoluments and capital incentives. There are also chapters dealing with social security contributions and benefits, and the advantages and disadvantages of being a self-employed (Schedule D) taxpayer as opposed to a Schedule E (employed) taxpayer.

Emotive Subject

This book is concerned not with politics but with the purely factual aspects of Schedule E taxation.

However, readers will appreciate that the subject is an emotive one, about which people tend to express extreme views. A good example of this is the following Parliamentary exchange, quoted in *Hansard* on December 18th, 1975:

> " Mr. Ashley: Is my hon. friend aware that we receive many loud complaints from wealthy Conservatives shouting through the windows of their Rolls-Royces about abuses of the tax system by people on unemployment pay and social security benefits? But is he aware of the abuses of the tax system by a large number of upper management who receive "perks" worth millions of pounds, including interest-free loans, housing, entertainment and a variety of other things? Does he realise that while the Chancellor does nothing the broadest backs get the biggest gift packages? Will he now stop acting as Santa Claus to these people and don the robe of Robin Hood?
>
> Mr. Davis: As my hon. friend says, there are abuses throughout the tax system and people at the higher levels have a better opportunity to reduce their tax burden than people at the lower levels. As I said, my right hon. friend (i.e. the Chancellor of the Exchequer) is looking at these matters urgently but I could not anticipate his Budget Statement."

Nowadays taxation dominates every business decision to an undesirable extent. Few commercial courses of action can now be embarked upon without first examining in great detail their possible taxation consequences. In the author's experience, the situation has deteriorated to the point where commercial men often consider the potential taxation consequences of a particular business decision before they analyse the broader financial and commercial implications. This is of course to approach the matter the wrong way round; in all cases commercial men must make their decisions without prior consideration of taxation. Once a decision has been made, on commercial terms, the tax adviser should be called in to see whether it can be modified in order to alleviate the tax burden, *but without upsetting the overall strategy*. Anyone who puts considerations of taxation before those of commerce is normally doomed to failure: it is far better to make a profit and pay some tax than to design the most sophisticated tax mitigation arrangement in the world and to make no commercial profits at all!

Topics not dealt with

This book is concerned with the taxation of the Schedule E taxpayer: the director and the employee. The subject is vast, and therefore the following areas cannot be dealt with:

i)   **Corporation Tax**

Generally speaking, all items of pay, directors' fees, benefits in kind and the like will be a good deduction In computing the company's own corporation tax liability. Having said that, it is clearly important to establish in every case whether a particular payment or benefit which may be tax efficient for the recipient director or employee is tax effective for the company as well. It would be wrong to assume automatically − particularly in the case of capital incentives given to Schedule E taxpayers − that every payment made by the company is necessarily a corporation tax deductible item, although the general rule is that any payments made for staff purposes ought to be treated as such. However, with corporation tax at 52% (or 42% for small companies) some employers may take the view that it is more tax efficient to mitigate the tax liability of the recipient director or employee, who is potentially taxable at up to 83%, than to obtain a deduction in the company's liability, where the relief is a maximum of 52%.

Any payment or benefit in kind should therefore always be analysed from the point of view both of corporation tax and of Schedule E.

ii)   **Pay Code**

Although the precise position regarding official pay policy is presently unclear, this book will not concern itself with discussing whether the introduction of a particular salary re-grading, benefit in kind, etc., may or may not be subject to any pay code restrictions. As a *general rule*, however, it can be said that the taxable value of a salary rise or benefit in kind is not necessarily the quantum of the benefit for pay code purposes. The Department of Employment has stated that for pay policy purposes the value will be calculated on the basis of the cash benefit to the recipient (which in the case of company cars, for instance, will not be the same as the taxable value).

iii)   **Staff Morale**

No attempt has been made to evaluate the 'incentive' effect on staff of a company providing a flexible emolument package. Nevertheless, this is an important consideration for any employer, since quite apart from the taxation implications certain employees may respond favourably if the company, as part of an overall package, provides them with benefits which they could not otherwise afford for themselves. Typical examples are the provision of an expensive motorcar for the sole use of the director or executive in question, or the opportunity to make use of, say, a company holiday home overseas. As a *quid pro quo* for the company providing such substantial benefits in kind, the direct cash salary paid could almost certainly be reduced.

Reason for Growth in Fringe Benefits

Several chapters of this book are devoted to fringe benefits: that is to say, the provision of benefits in kind such as motorcars, cheap housing, nil or low interest rate loans, free medical assistance, etc.

A major reason for the substantial growth in recent years in the provision of benefits in kind for directors and employees must surely be the UK's high marginal tax rates, whereby income tax can rise to 83% on *taxable* incomes in excess of £21,000 per annum. For those taxpayers in receipt of investment income, the marginal rate rises to 98%.

In terms of overall taxation — even if the benefit were to be entirely

taxable and regarded as part of the director's/employee's emoluments —
it is almost invariably cheaper to give a benefit in kind rather than
cash. This principle will be illustrated in subsequent chapters.

International Comparisons

It is perhaps inappropriate for a book of this kind to comment on the
disparity between the net salaries enjoyed in the UK and those received
in other civilised Western countries. Nevertheless, it must be said that
with a weak pound, high inflation and high taxation, executives in this
country are generally much worse off than taxpayers holding comparable positions overseas. This is so even if the higher cost of living
generally experienced overseas is taken into account.

When considering our EEC colleagues, it is an inescapable fact that
marginal tax rates in the UK (at 83%) are substantially higher than
those in, say, West Germany (56%) or France (60%). Even the comparison of tax rates is an over-simplification, since one must also
consider which deductions and allowances may be used in computing
the *taxable income* on which the tax burden ultimately falls. To take
one illustration, Holland has a fairly high marginal tax rate, but Dutch
taxpayers can, for example, freely deduct interest payments when
calculating their taxable income, whereas most readers will be aware
that — with the exception of specific items like interest on a mortgage
not exceeding £25,000 — the UK taxpayers' right to deduct interest
payments for tax purposes is severely curtailed.

Definitions

As far as possible the author wishes to avoid technical jargon, which
though it may well be a satisfactory method of communication between
taxation experts, merely serves to confuse many readers. Unfortunately,
taxation is a highly technical subject and it is important that readers be
aware of the precise meaning of certain words and phrases. The
following should be particularly noted:

i)   "Resident"

As far as this book is concerned, perhaps the most important of these words is 'resident'. Although the term appears frequently in taxation statutes, there is unfortunately no statutory definition of it. One must therefore consider the everyday meaning of the word, as amplified first by the Courts' decisions, and secondly — and in practice perhaps more importantly — by Inland Revenue interpretation.

Since taxation is an annual tax, one must consider whether a particular person can be said to be resident in the UK during a particular tax year (from 6th April to the following 5th April). In order to be regarded as resident, that person must usually be physically present in the UK for at least part of the year. In practice this means that:

a) A person will always be resident in the UK if he is physically present for more than 6 months during the fiscal year — 6 months being regarded as equivalent to 183 days, whether or not the year is a leap year. Although for this purpose present Revenue practice usually ignores the days of arrival in and departure from the UK, all the days spent in the UK during the fiscal year must be aggregated; that is to say, the test is *not* one of consecutive days, but of aggregate days.

It must be emphasised that the use of the term 'resident' for income tax purposes is entirely independent of whether a person is 'resident' for exchange control purposes in the eyes of the Bank of England. The two are entirely unconnected, and much confusion can arise over this point when discussing taxpayers working for a period outside the UK (see chapter 9 for further details).

b) If a person does not spend more than 6 months during the year in the UK, he can nevertheless still be resident here if he visits the UK on an *habitual* basis. In practice, this means that if a person visits the UK for an average of at least 3 months per fiscal year over a 4-year period, then THEREAFTER he will be regarded as resident in the UK for tax purposes. However if it is clear when that person first comes to the UK that he proposes making visits of this nature in the future, the Revenue may well treat him as resident (and indeed 'ordinarily resident') in the UK from the outset.

c) If a person has a place of abode available for his use in the UK, then mere physical presence for only 1 day during the tax year can mean that he is regarded as resident here. Whether or not a place of abode can be said to be 'available' for use is a question of fact, but the general rule of thumb is that if the individual has the key to the door and can come and go as he pleases, then in taxation terms he almost certainly has a place of abode available for his use. Certainly the taxpayer need not own the property in question before he can be regarded as having it 'available' for his use.

The vast majority of readers will, of course, be resident in the UK for tax purposes.

ii) "Ordinarily Resident"

In the same way as the preceding, there is no statutory definition of this term and one must therefore fall back on commonsense, Court rulings and Inland Revenue interpretations.

The term "ordinarily resident" is broadly equivalent to habitually resident; that is to say, if a person is resident in the UK year after year he is ordinarily resident here as well.

In certain circumstances a person can be resident in the UK (i.e. if he visits the UK for more than 6 months during the tax year) but not ordinarily resident in the UK, since he normally lives overseas. Conversely, if a person who usually lives in the UK goes abroad for, say, a long holiday and does not come back to the UK during the tax year, then that person would be regarded as remaining ordinarily resident in the UK, although not resident for that particular fiscal year of absence.

iii) "Domicile"

The main importance of this concept is in determining capital transfer tax liability, and therefore it is of little relevance to a book on Schedule E. However, the term will be used in Chapter 9 and therefore a brief definition is called for.

Whereas the terms 'resident' and 'ordinarily resident' are questions of fact, a person's 'domicile' is a question of intention. Furthermore, a person can only have one domicile at any one time, whereas a taxpayer may be resident or ordinarily resident in both the UK and an overseas country during the same year.

Briefly, a person's domicile is the place which he regards as his natural home, and to which he ultimately intends to return, although he may be away from it for quite substantial periods of time. At birth the taxpayer acquires a domicile of *origin*, which normally corresponds with the domicile of the child's father, except in certain circumstances such as illegitimate births, when the child's domicile corresponds with that of the mother.

Once acquired, a domicile of origin is hard to shake off. A new 'domicile of choice' can be acquired, but this involves proving a change in intention. Quite dramatic changes in lifestyle are required in order to demonstrate that a person with a UK domicile of origin intends giving that up in favour of a new overseas domicile of choice. As an example of how difficult it can be to renounce one's domicile of origin, readers are referred to the case of IRC v. Bullock, determined in the Court of Appeal and reported in *The Times* on 25th June 1976.

iv)   "United Kingdom"

The United Kingdom comprises England, Wales, Scotland and Northern Ireland. It does NOT include the Channel Islands or the Isle of Man. Thus the term 'abroad' or 'overseas' should be interpreted as meaning outside the UK (i.e. Jersey is 'overseas' and a person working in Jersey is working 'abroad' for the purposes of this book).

It must be emphasised that the above definitions are somewhat cursory, owing to the pressures of space.

Professional Advice

The bulk of this book is devoted to analysing the new Schedule E regulations introduced in the 1976 and 1977 Finance Acts. These rules are new and therefore have not been subjected to judicial scrutiny or consideration.

The views expressed in this book are solely those of the author, based on his understanding of the law and current practice in this area.

While the book seeks to provide an up-to-date analysis of Schedule E taxation and to put forward certain ideas relating to tax planning, it can be no substitute for good professional advice based on the circumstances of the individual case. It must therefore be stressed that any company or individual Schedule E taxpayer contemplating a particular course of action should seek competent professional advice before doing so, and should not base their plans, ideas or schemes solely on this book.

CHAPTER 2

FUNDAMENTALS OF SCHEDULE E TAXATION

Before examining the intricacies of executive remuneration, it is necessary to understand the basic fundamentals of Schedule E taxation. It is of great importance to establish that the particular source of income under scrutiny is a Schedule E source and not a Schedule D source, and this chapter shows how to distinguish one from the other.

It is also necessary to explain the meaning of the word "emoluments" and to detail some of the deductions which are allowable for Schedule E purposes in computing final tax liability. Finally, comment needs to be made on the method of tax collection of Schedule E liability — known as Pay As You Earn.

For convenience therefore this chapter has been split into the following parts:

PART I	—	WHAT IS AN EMPLOYMENT?
PART II	—	SCHEDULE E CASES I, II AND III
PART III	—	WHAT ARE "EMOLUMENTS"?
PART IV	—	DEDUCTIONS ALLOWED
PART V	—	PAYE SYSTEM

PART I – WHAT IS AN EMPLOYMENT?

Introduction

As a starting point, it is vital to draw a distinction between Schedule E and Schedule D taxpayers. The Schedule E taxpayer holds an office or employment and is thus chargeable to tax (usually through the PAYE system) under Schedule E. A person who is self employed (e.g. a sole trader, a partner and the like) is taxable under Schedule D.

Type of Contract

The usual distinction between Schedule E and Schedule D is that the former is a contract *of* service and the latter is a contract *for* services. This is illustrated by the comment of Lord Denning in the case of Stevenson Jordan and Harrison Limited v. Macdonald and Evans (1952): "A ship's master, a chauffeur and a reporter of a newspaper are all employed under a contract of service — so they are Schedule E people. But a ship's pilot, a taxi man and a newspaper contributor are employed under a contract for services — thus Schedule D".

In the past, the main single factor in determining whether a contract is "of" service or "for" service has been the degree of control exercisable. A Schedule E taxpayer who is employed under a contract of service will have to follow the directions of his employer whereas a Schedule D taxpayer who has a contract for services is usually free to perform the contract in the most appropriate way he or she thinks fit. However, with the increasing degree of technical and professional skill required in so many activities, the old traditional test of control is being found inadequate in more recent cases. Nowadays the test of being employed under a contract of service depends not so much on whether the employee submits to orders but more on whether he is "part and parcel" of the organisation. Factors to be taken into account would include:

i) The degree of integration into the business or organisation.

ii) The particular terms of the individual contract.

iii) Whether or not the person concerned is in business on his own account.

iv) The degree of control exercised over that person.

Cases

1. In the case of Argent v. Minister of Social Security (1968) an

actor, who was also a part time teacher of music and drama at a school, was held *not* to be an employed person. The actor had a reasonably free choice of what he taught and an entirely free choice of how he taught it. He was paid at a rate per hour or at a particular fee for a particular job.

The Judge held that no *single factor* could be decisive. All the facts had to be examined and in the particular circumstances of the case it was quite unreal to say that the actor was employed under a contract of service.

2.   However, a part time interviewer employed by a market research agency had a series of separate contracts, each for a specified survey. On the particular facts of that case it was held that the part time interviewer was employed under a series of such contracts of service and was thus an employed person — Market Investigations Limited v. Minister of Social Security (1969).

Part of Professional Activities

It is common for a person — in pursuit of his profession or vocation — to enter into a long series of contracts and engagements with different people. In circumstances of this nature it has to be decided whether any of these contracts or engagements are contracts of service or pertain to the holding of an office, in which case they would be assessable under Schedule E, with only the remaining contracts or engagements being assessable under Schedule D. Alternatively, it may be that none of the particular contracts or engagements are offices or employments in which case they would all be assessable under the provisions of Schedule D.

In every case, the following question must therefore be asked — Does the taxpayer, in respect of a particular activity:

a)   Occupy an office,

b)   undertake an employment, or

c)   does he merely render services in the course of the exercise or practice of his profession?

Once it has been decided that a particular activity is a source of profit assessable under Schedule E or Schedule D then that source must be assessed in accordance with the rules applicable to the appropriate Schedule. It is not permissible to set off the deductions allowed under one Schedule against a particular source of income which is assessable under the other. There are a number of leading authorities on this point and in 1960 several cases (e.g. Mitchell and Eden v. Ross) were taken dealing with specialist medical consultants who held part time appointments on various regional hospital boards under the National Health Service Act 1946.

In each case, the consultants rendered services to patients under the Act and received fees in respect thereof from the particular hospital board by which they were appointed. The point at issue was whether the profits or gains arising from such appointments were profits or gains arising from an office or employment — and thus taxable under Schedule E — or whether they were profits or gains arising from the exercise of the profession and thus taxable under Schedule D Case II. In every case the Courts held that each specialist consultant was *properly* described as the holder of an office in respect of the part time employment and he was thus properly assessable under Schedule E in respect of the profits or gains from those appointments (including any locum tenens work).

The Court further held that in so far as an expense incurred in relation to the employments was *not* deductible under the Schedule E rules, the consultants were not entitled to deduct the expense under Schedule D since the two Schedules are mutually exclusive, even though the holding of the part time employment was a necessary part of the exercise of the profession. Thus the taxpayer had two distinct sources of income and the expenses of the office (Schedule E) could not be regarded as deductible in computing the profits of the profession (Schedule D).

Summary

From the foregoing, it will be seen to be a question of degree and fact whether a taxpayer with two or more sources of income is:

a)   employed in one or more employments (Schedule E)

b)   exercising one or more professions or vocations (Schedule D)

c)   involved in a combination of (a) and (b).

In certain situations specific fiscal legislation seeks to alter the classification of a particular income source. For example, as a result of Section 38 F.A. (No. 2) 1975, those termed "workers supplied through agencies" are to be regarded as Schedule E and not Schedule D taxpayers from 6th April 1976 onwards. Before this change in the law, people such as temporary secretaries regarded themselves as Schedule D "freela ce" taxpayers.

PART II – SCHEDULE E CASES I, II AND III

Introduction

Having established that a particular source of income or profit is a source of Schedule E income, the particular circumstances must be considered to see under which *Case* the employment income falls. Schedule E is divided into three Cases, depending on the residential status of the employee and the place where the duties are performed.

Case I

Where the person holding the office or employment is resident and ordinarily resident in the UK, any emoluments received are chargeable to tax – subject to a deduction/exemption if the emoluments are "foreign emoluments" and subject to the appropriate deduction/ exemption specified in the 1977 Finance Act if the employee performs duties wholly or partly outside the UK.

Case II

Case II applies where the person is not resident or, if he is resident, then not ordinarily resident in the UK. In this circumstance, he is taxable on any emoluments for the fiscal year in respect of duties performed in the UK (but subject to an appropriate deduction if the emoluments in question are "foreign emoluments").

Case III

Where a person is resident in the UK, he can be taxable on any emoluments received in the UK in the fiscal year, being emoluments either for that period *or* for an earlier period for which he has been resident there, and likewise on any emoluments for that period received in the UK in an earlier period.

Further Observations

The following further observations are relevant to Cases I, II and III:

a)   For Case I to apply, the employee must be *both* resident and ordinarily resident in the UK for the fiscal year in question. If he fulfills these conditions, then he is fully taxable (subject to allowable deductions specified later) on his worldwide income.

Although he is taxable on the full income *arising* in the tax year, a certain measure of relief is available if the emoluments either constitute foreign emoluments *or* if all or part of the duties thereof are performed outside the UK. These two aspects will be considered in Chapter 9.

b)   Case II applies where either the person is not resident *or* (if he is resident) then not ordinarily resident in the UK. In such circumstances, he is taxable on what may loosely be termed his UK source income. This is fully taxable on an arising basis but subject again to a measure of relief if the emoluments constitute foreign emoluments as will be explained in Chapter 9.

It is perhaps important to emphasise that the relief given to duties performed wholly or partly overseas introduced by Finance Act 1977 is *not* relevant to Schedule E Case II. The relief is only available to taxpayers falling within Schedule E Case I.

c)   Case III is a sweeping up Case designed to levy a tax charge on
      income which for some reason has not come within the previous
      two Cases. As will be seen, Case III income is taxable on what
      may be termed a remittances basis and not (as in the other two
      Cases) on an arising basis.

Example

      David Jones is resident (but not ordinarily resident nor domi-
      ciled) for tax purposes in the UK. He has a job with Westward
      Ho Television in Liechtenstein, no duties of which are per-
      formed in the UK. David earns the equivalent of £10,000 a
      year.
      Provided David does not remit any of the overseas earnings
      to the UK, he will not be taxable since he cannot be brought
      within the provisions of Cases I or II of Schedule E. However,
      if David ever *remits* any of the overseas earnings from
      Westward Ho Television to the UK, a tax charge will arise by
      virtue of Schedule E Case III.

d)   Readers are referred to the definitions contained in Chapter 1 to
      explain the terms "resident", "ordinarily resident", "domicile"
      and "UK".

e)   It should be noted that certain duties of an office or employment
      under the Crown of a public nature are regarded as being per-
      formed in the UK even though as a matter of fact the duties may
      be performed outside the UK.

PART III – WHAT ARE "EMOLUMENTS"?

Introduction

Tax is charged under Cases I, II or III of Schedule E on the full amount
of the "emoluments" from the office or employment. The expression
"emoluments" is defined (Section 183 (1) T.A.1970) as including "all
salaries, fees, wages, perquisites and profits whatsoever".

Although emoluments usually consist primarily of money, other items can fall within the classification of emoluments and these are dealt with below. One further area of emoluments is benefits in kind (or fringe benefits) and the taxation of these will be discussed in detail in Chapter 3.

In every case one must consider the nature of the payment and *not necessarily* the identity of payer. Furthermore, a payment is treated as an emolument even if it is called something different — e.g. a "cost of living bonus".

Gifts

A payment may have no direct connection with the taxpayer's remuneration or employment at all and therefore will not be in the nature of an emolument.

The fact that there is some link between the payment and the employment — and indeed that the payment would never have been made but for the employment — is not sufficient to render the payment *automatically* taxable (e.g. Hochstrasser v. Mayes (1960)). However, it will be taxable if it is paid to the employee as a reward for or in return for acting as or being an employee.

Tips

People in certain trades — e.g. restaurant and hotel employees, taxi drivers and railway porters — receive tips which form a substantial part of their income. In the case of Calvert v. Wainwright (1947) a taxi driver was assessed to Schedule E tax in respect of tips received *even though*, firstly, his employer gave evidence that the taxi driver was employed at a particular wage and tips were not part of the bargain, and, secondly, the tips were not paid by his employer but by customers. On the particular facts of the case the Courts held that the tips were emoluments but it was stated that any sums given as a *present* in appreciation of the recipient's personal qualities (such as faithfulness, consistency and readiness to oblige) would not be taxable under Schedule E.

Tax Free Remuneration

Any agreement to pay salaries or wages without deduction of income
tax or "free" of income tax is not effective since the recipient employee
will be regarded — for tax purposes — as having received gross emoluments equivalent to the amount actually received by the employee plus
the tax paid on his behalf by the employer (North British Rail Co. v.
Scott 1923).

Readers will appreciate that, as far as directors are concerned, payment of tax free remuneration is specifically prohibited under the
Companies Act legislation.

Company Shares

It is uncommon to find Schedule E taxpayers receiving — as part of
their emoluments — free entitlements to shares. The majority of share
option or share incentive schemes involve the granting of some right to
acquire share option or shares on particular terms and this topic is
covered in Chapter 7.

However, if a free entitlement to shares is given, then the value of
that right or entitlement will be taxable at *outset* as part of the emoluments of the recipient under the ordinary Schedule E principles.

Likewise, if a director or employee is offered shares at less than
their market value, he will, if he accepts the offer, be liable to tax
under Schedule E at outset on the difference between the consideration
he gives for them and the market value. This was considered in the case
of Weight v. Salmon (1935). The Managing Director of the company
was entitled to a fixed salary under his service contract. In addition the
directors of the company (by resolution each year) gave him the
privilege of subscribing at par for certain unissued shares of the
company. The market value of the shares so subscribed was substantially in excess of par and the Crown succeeded in their contention
that the difference between these two figures represented a taxable
emolument under Schedule E.

Where a Schedule E taxpayer voluntarily applies part of his emoluments to the acquisition of company shares (albeit on arms length
commercial terms) he will nevertheless be taxable on the emoluments

so applied. In the case of Parker v. Chapman (1928) the taxpayer was entitled to certain commission earnings from his company. The company announced a new issue of shares and the taxpayer agreed to take up additional shares and to apply the commission due to him in part payment thereof. The taxpayer claimed that as his commission was not payable in cash but in shares and that as the shares had always been unrealisable and had no present value, he should not be taxable on them. The Court of Appeal held that in the circumstances the company was under an obligation to pay him commission and the fact that he *voluntarily* applied the commission to buy shares was his own choice. The commission was thus properly taxable under Schedule E.

If a person receives shares as part and parcel of his emoluments, he will be taxable on the value received. Otherwise, if he acquires shares (or share options) by virtue of this employment, he potentially comes within the ambit of the special rules applicable to share option and incentive schemes discussed in Chapter 7.

Extra Statutory Concessions

From time to time the Revenue announce what are termed extra statutory concessions whereby they abandon or modify their entitlement to levy tax in particular circumstances.

Some such concessions apply to Schedule E, for example:

i) Where a miner (entitled to receive free coal) opts for cash in lieu of the coal, the Revenue will not assess such cash payments as emoluments for Schedule E purposes. The cash (and for that matter the coal if taken) is tax free.

ii) Income tax is not charged on the value of luncheon vouchers issued to employees provided:

    a) The vouchers are non-transferable and used for meals only, *and*

    b) *if* any restriction is placed on their issue to employees, the luncheon vouchers must be available to lower paid staff, *and*

c)   the value of vouchers does not exceed 15p for each working day. If they do exceed 15p, then only the first 15p is tax free.

Living Accommodation Provided for Employees

The whole taxation position in this area has been recast by Section 33 of the 1977 Finance Act. The tax provisions apply to all employees — not merely those subject to the more penal benefit in kind rules which will be described in detail in Chapter 4.

In essence, where an employee is provided with living accommodation, he stands to be taxable on an amount equal to the annual value of the property *less* any contribution made by the employee. The term "annual value" means the *rateable value* of the property as defined in Section 531 T.A.1970. (An illustration of this principle as applied to an executive is given in Chapter 5).

However, if the employer himself rents the property (as opposed to buying it) and makes the property available rent free to the employee then the employee will be taxable by reference to the actual amount of rent paid by the employer *if* this is higher than the annual value.

There are, however, three situations when a person can occupy property rent free without the benefit thereof being chargeable to income tax as an emolument under Schedule E:

i)   Where it is *necessary* for the *proper performance* of the employee's duties that he should reside in the accommodation (e.g. office caretakers, lighthouse keepers, etc.).

ii)   Where the accommodation is provided for the *better performance* of the duties of the employment and the employment in question is one of those where it is *customary* for employers to provide living accommodation for employees. (This provision is completely new and it may take some time before the full impact of it is completely appreciated. Initially it was introduced to cover the position of policemen living in police houses but the clause may well have a somewhat wider impact).

iii)   Where there is a special threat to a person's security and special security arrangements are in force which involve the employee in residing in accommodation belonging to the employer. (This was initially drafted so as to benefit Government employees only, but now — in theory at least — the exemption is available to anyone who can show some special threat to his security).

Although any company employee may come within the scope of the exemptions, exemptions (i) and (ii) above will *not* be available to a company *director* unless that director fulfills two conditions. Firstly, the director must either be a full time working director or he must work for a non-profit making or charitable concern and secondly he must not be "interested" in more than 5% of the company's equity.

It is specifically provided that accommodation made available for the employee's spouse and members of his family or household will be taxable as if made available to the employee in person.

Generally speaking all living accommodation provided by an employer is regarded as having been provided by reason of the employment and is thus potentially taxable on the Schedule E taxpayer concerned. There are certain minor exceptions to this rule relating to individual employers and accommodation provided by local authorities in specified circumstances (i.e. council houses).

PART IV — DEDUCTIONS ALLOWED

Introduction

Income tax is levied not on the gross income derived by the employee under Schedule E, but on the net income after deduction of expenses. Whether or not a particular expense can be properly deducted under Schedule E depends on whether it falls within the provisions of Section 189 T.A.1970. For the expense to fall within this Section, it must be "wholly, exclusively and *necessarily*" incurred in the performance of the duties. The major problem relates to the word "necessarily" and in many cases which have come before the Courts, the inclusion of the word "necessarily" has served to nullify the deductibility of a particular payment.

Case

The expense claim rules are notoriously rigid and restrictive in their operation and this can be illustrated by quoting part of the judgement in the case of Lomax v. Newton (1953) — "An expenditure may be "necessary" for the holder of an office without being necessary to him in the performance of the duties of that office; it may be necessary in the performance of those duties without being exclusively referable to those duties; it may perhaps be both necessarily and exclusively, but still not wholly so referable. The words are indeed stringent and exacting; compliance with each and every one of them is obligatory if the benefit of (Section 189) is to be claimed successfully".

Expenses of Obtaining Employment

These are not deductible. In the case of Henderson Short v. McIlgorm (1945) a taxpayer had obtained a position through an employment agency to which he paid a fee of £30. The claim to deduct this fee when computing the tax liability was turned down because the expense could not be held to have been incurred in the performance of the duties.

Professional Subscriptions

Annual subscriptions or fees paid to a professional body or learned society approved by the Inland Revenue is an allowable deduction for Schedule E purposes provided the activities are *relevant* to the office or employment.

Plant and Machinery

In certain cases where a taxpayer buys plant and machinery (as defined for tax purposes) for use in the office or employment, he may be entitled firstly to claim capital allowances in respect of the purchase price and, secondly, may be able to claim interest on any money borrowed to buy the plant or machinery for at least 3 full fiscal years.

Travelling Expenses

Expenses of travelling from home to the place of work are not deduct-ible because they are not incurred in the performance of the duties of the office or employment. For example, in the case of Cook v. Knott (1887) the taxpayer was a solicitor at Worcester and also a clerk to the Justices at Bromyard. He claimed to deduct the cost of travelling between Worcester and Bromyard. The Court held that the expenses were not admissible because the place where a man chooses to live is entirely up to him and travelling from where he lives to the place he discharges his duties cannot be said to be in the performance of those duties. This principle has been upheld on many occasions since then. (See also note 11 (iii) in Chapter 5).

Travelling in the course of the duties of the employment are of course tax deductible since they are incurred in the performance of the duties in question. If the employer reimburses these expenses, such reimbursement will not be taxable as part of the employee's Schedule E income.

Clothing

On many occasions it has been held that the cost of buying ordinary clothing cannot be deductible in computing Schedule E income tax liability. However, if the employee has to acquire special clothing — e.g. protective clothing — a claim for a deduction in Schedule E income tax liability is allowed. In certain industries, a fixed level of clothing allowance has been agreed with the Inland Revenue.

Finance Act 1977

Although not strictly relevant to expenses for Schedule E purposes, it should be noted that the 1977 Finance Act has extended the right of certain employees with "job related" employments to claim relief for interest paid on a mortgage to buy their own house. This will be a benefit to employees such as lighthouse keepers, caretakers and the like who have to live on the premises but who may wish to buy a house for their retirement. Hitherto they have been denied relief on such mortgage interest.

The provision giving this new relief is contained in Section 36 Finance Act 1977. The wording of this Section is similar to that used for the three exemptions (listed earlier) given under Section 33 Finance Act 1977, whereby certain categories of Schedule E taxpayer residing in living accommodation provided for them by their employer are not taxable on this benefit. (That is to say if it is for the proper performance of the duties, if it is for the better performance of the duties, and if a special threat to security exists).

Unfortunately this relief has not been given retrospectively and only interest paid on or after 6th April 1977 will qualify.

PART V – PAYE SYSTEM

Introduction

The Pay As You Earn (PAYE) system applies to all Schedule E emoluments. It thus applies not only to weekly wages but also to monthly salaries, annual salaries, bonuses, commissions, directors' fees, pensions and any other income from an office or employment.

The intention of the provisions is to spread the income tax charge over the year and to collect tax from Schedule E taxpayers on a regular basis as and when they receive their pay.

Coding Notice

Every year Schedule E taxpayers receive a tax form from the Inland Revenue on which they should list their various personal entitlements – e.g. married allowance, single person's allowance, life assurance premium relief mortgage interest, alimony payments and the like – and this form will be returned to the tax office. THIS INFORMATION IS NEVER DIVULGED TO THE EMPLOYER.

From the information received by the tax office, the Inland Revenue will allocate the employee a code number. This code number depends directly on the allowances claimed. For example, if the employee claims total allowances of, say, £1,950, his code number will be "195". If the employee is only a single person with no allowances (and thus entitled only to the single person's allowance of £845 in 1977/78) his code number will be "84". In every case the code number is ascertained by adding up the total allowances and then deleting the last figure. With the actual code number there is usually a letter suffixed or prefixed (or in some cases a combination of both). All these letters denote a particular category of employee.

The most common suffixes found in practice are H (married allowance), L (single person's or wife's earnings allowance), P (full single *age* allowance) or V (full married *age* allowance). The object of these codes is that should the personal allowances be changed in a Budget the tax office can immediately identify who is entitled to the increased allowances and can pass the increases on to the taxpayer without delay. Taxpayers who have the suffix "T" or the prefix "F" have to be reviewed individually by the tax office and these taxpayers normally have to wait a little longer to receive any benefit from the increased tax allowances.

Thus the notice of coding depends directly on the allowances to which the Schedule E taxpayer is entitled. A proportion of these allowances is set against his pay each normal pay day.

Employer

The burden of the PAYE system is thrown onto employers who are obliged to calculate the tax liability of their employees each pay day and to account to the Inland Revenue on a regular basis for the income tax deducted. To enable them to do this they are allocated each year:

i)   Deduction Cards

ii)   Coding notices for employees

iii)   Tax Tables

Should the reader require a detailed exposition of the intricate workings of the PAYE system as it affects the employer he should obtain a free copy of the Inland Revenue booklet P7 — "Employer's Guide to PAYE".

Common Forms

A large number of forms are in use in the PAYE system, but perhaps -the following are the best known by Schedule E taxpayers:

i)   **Form P45**

A person leaving service is given a certificate (on form P45) containing various particulars. The form records the national insurance number and also the employee's tax code (including the appropriate alphabetical suffix or prefix). Form P45 will also be used on the death of an employee or on the employee's retirement (unless, in the latter case, he receives a pension paid by the *former employer*).

Part 1 of Form P45 should be sent by the employer to the tax office immediately. Parts 2 and 3 of the form are handed to the employee when he leaves. On no account should an employer supply duplicates of Parts 2 and 3 of Form P45 to an employee who has left the employment but has lost the originals.

When the employee starts his new job, his new employer will ask him for Parts 2 and 3 of form P45. The new employer should follow the instructions on Part 2 of the form and send part 3 to his local tax office. A tax deduction card should also be prepared. If for any reason the employee does not produce a form P45 to the new employer then the employer should send form P46 to the local tax office immediately and prepare a deduction card for the new employee using the emergency code. This will classify the new employee as a single person with no other allowances and tax will be deducted by the new employer by reference to this code until he receives further instructions from the tax office (by Form P6). When this information is received from the tax office the details should be entered onto the Deduction Card.

ii)   **Form P60**

After April 5th each year an employer is required to give a certificate to each employee who was in his employment on that date and from whose pay tax has been deducted. The certificate must show the following information:

a)   employer's name and address

b)   employee's name and national insurance number

c)   tax office reference

d)   code at 5th April

e)   total pay for tax purposes received during the year together with actual tax paid by the employee

f)   pay and tax deducted in previous employments included on the employer's Deduction Card.

Alterations to entries on form P60 should not be made. If an error is made a new certificate must be prepared and the incorrect one destroyed. Duplicate certificates are not to be issued and any employee who asks for a duplicate should be referred to the local tax office.

iii)   **Form P11D**

Where the employer is deducting tax for a director or employee whose emoluments are at the rate of £5,000 a year or more (see Chapter 3, Part II for further particulars) the employer should also complete form P11D. This form should be in the Inspector of Taxes' hands by 6th May immediately following the end of the tax year. Form P11D shows all expense payments and the cost of all benefits and facilities provided for the Schedule E taxpayer except those within the limits of any "dispensation".

The special rules applicable to the taxation of benefits in kind (explained in detail in Chapter 4) are not aimed at expenses, payments or benefits the cost of which would be allowable as an income tax expense. If, therefore, the employer provides the Inspector of Taxes with full particulars of the benefits supplied, and the particular circumstances when the benefits are made available, the Inspector will (if he is satisfied that they are of a reasonable scale and genuinely relate to business) issue a "dispensation" to the effect that any payments covered by the dispensation need not be included on form P11D.

Pay

PAYE income tax is deducted on a regular basis throughout the year as and when pay is received. The amount of pay, however, from which tax is deducted is not the gross pay but the pay after making allowance for any tax deductible pension scheme contributions which may be paid. It should be noted that employers are also responsible for deducting employees' (and their own) national insurance contributions and that this is now all part of the PAYE system. The only distinction is that the national insurance contributions must be calculated by reference to gross pay and not pay as reduced by allowable pension scheme contributions as is the case for the ascertainment of tax liability.

CHAPTER 3

AN INTRODUCTION TO FRINGE BENEFITS

The previous chapter gave a general outline of the Schedule E basis of taxation: what constitutes an "employment", the amount on which income tax is levied, and how the income tax liability is collected by the Inland Revenue through the PAYE system.

The provision of non-cash benefits such as living accommodation, medical benefits, school fees and company cars is increasingly being considered as a possible way of alleviating income tax liability. This chapter therefore seeks to outline the taxation basis of non-cash emoluments in general terms, and to explain the distinction which the tax legislation draws, in taxing benefits in kind, between certain classes of Schedule E taxpayer.

Generally speaking employers in other Western countries do not provide such an elaborate package of potential benefits in kind for their employees. This is primarily because income tax is somewhat lower and thus there is less incentive to provide emoluments in anything other than cash form. Another reason may be that overseas tax laws on benefits in kind are rather harsher than those applicable in the UK. Only a few years ago, many of the American companies establishing operations in the UK were puzzled as to why UK staff were not satisfied with substantial cash emoluments and no benefits in kind, since the US employer is mainly accustomed to providing cash "which the executive can spend how he wants", not a whole range of fringe benefits. By now, however, most American parent companies have come to appreciate the peculiar problems of the UK tax system and seem prepared to provide tax efficient overall emolument packages (see Chapter 5 for further comment).

This chapter is an introduction to the general topic of fringe benefits, and it has been split into the following two parts:

PART I – GENERAL LEGAL POSITION OF BENEFITS IN
KIND

PART II – PROBLEMS OF DIRECTORS AND HIGHER PAID
STAFF

PART I – GENERAL LEGAL POSITION OF BENEFITS IN KIND

Introduction

Chapter 2 analysed in considerable detail the scope of Schedule E
income tax and explained that it was levied on all emoluments which
can properly be said to emanate from the office or employment.
Specific rules, such as those applicable to rent free accommodation
provided by the employer, were also explained.

Valuation of Benefits in Kind

Where an employee receives some recompense other than cash (popularly termed a "fringe benefit" or a "benefit in kind"), that benefit may
be regarded as an emolument within the scope of Schedule E.

However, the *value* of that emolument for taxation purposes must
be considered before it is possible to analyse the taxation consequence.

The general valuation rule for benefits in kind was stated by Lord
Halsbury in the case of Tennant v. Smith (1892): "I come to the
conclusion that the Act refers to money payments made to the person
who receives them though, of course, I do not deny that if substantial
things of money value were capable of being turned into money they
might for that purpose represent money's worth and therefore be
taxable".

In the same case, Lord Macnaghten said "On examining that
Schedule [i.e. Schedule E] it became obvious that it extends only to
money payments or payments convertible into money".

It follows from the above statements that if some non-convertible amenitv or benefit is made available to an employee, then that amenity or benefit is not *as a matter of general law* taxable on the employee as an emolument under Schedule E.

Example

Raymond Bloch, leading journalist with Tax Avoidance News, is paid £4,000 a year salary. To ensure his smart appearance, the magazine pays for him to have his hair cut on a regular basis; this costs £100 over the fiscal year.

Since Mr. Bloch is clearly not in a position to convert his haircut into a cash sum, this benefit in kind will be entirely free of Schedule E tax. THIS IS SO EVEN THOUGH, FIRSTLY, HIS EMPLOYER HAS CLEARLY INCURRED A COST IN THE PROVISION OF THE BENEFIT AND, SECONDLY, HAD THEY PAID HIM AN INCREASED SALARY WHICH HE IN TURN SPENT ON HAIRCUTS, THIS INCREASED SALARY WOULD HAVE BORNE TAX IN THE ORDINARY WAY.

Where a fringe benefit can be converted into cash, it will be subject to a Schedule E tax charge. However, the charge will be levied on the monetary amount which can be received by the disposal of the benefit; the *cost* of the benefit is quite irrelevant.

Example

Danby Godfrey, a printer who works for Big Block Printing, is given two free suits a year by his firm.

The suits cost the company £100 each and since they are in Mr. Godfrey's absolute ownership he is clearly in a position to obtain a cash sum for them. However, for taxation purposes one must ask "What can he receive for them?" The simple answer is "What he could reasonably sell them for in the open market." The open market price of Mr. Godfrey's suit may well be only £10, and if so he will be taxable on this £10 "cash-in" value rather than the original cost to his employer.

To summarise, the general rule is that if a benefit cannot be converted into cash it is free of tax, whereas if it does have a cash conversion value it is taxable on the employee to the amount of cash he or she may reasonably expect to receive on disposal. The cost to the employer is as such not relevant.

Danger Areas

Having stated the general principle, two potential danger areas must be pointed out:

i)   Firstly, the Courts have sometimes taken a rather interesting view of whether a benefit can properly be said to be convertible into cash. A good illustration is the case of Heaton v. Bell (1968). Briefly, the facts of the case were that an employee received a fixed salary but had the option of accepting a somewhat reduced salary and at the same time receiving a company car from the employer. If for any reason the employee no longer wanted a company car, he could give two weeks' notice to the employer, who would take the car back and restore the employee's old salary. For example, if the employee earned £2,000 but accepted a company car his salary would drop to £1,700. Were the car to be handed back to the employer, the employee's salary would revert to its original figure of £2,000 per annum.

In these circumstances the House of Lords held that the car *did* have a cash-in value, since the employee could receive extra emoluments simply by relinquishing the car and thus automatically reverting to his old salary level. The cash-in value was therefore held to be (on the figures illustrated) £300.

Provided the possibility of this type of judgement is borne in mind, no problems should arise. However, any employment contract which gives the employee a choice between salary or fringe benefits should be avoided if possible. Under the normal Schedule E rules, the provision of a company car to an employee should *not* be taxable as a benefit in kind, since the car remains the employer's property and therefore the employee cannot be said to be able to convert the benefit into cash. However, as will be explained later in this chapter and in Chapter 4, certain categories of employee are taxable on company cars even though they are not in a position to obtain cash for them.

ii) On no account must the employer ever take over a pecuniary liability of the employee. If he does so, this will be regarded as a taxable emolument.

Example

John Nixon, who works for Manchester Burnley & London Insurance Services Limited, runs up a personal bill of £200 in Mount Street Wine Bar.

His employers wish to provide John with some benefits in kind and therefore offer to take over the obligation to pay this personal bill.

Since John initially incurred the bill, his employers, by taking over the payment of it, are discharging a pecuniary liability of his. John will therefore be taxable on the full amount of the debt discharged; *even though*, had the employer himself been responsible for the bill at the outset, the fringe benefit may have been free of income tax under Schedule E.

Recent Developments

Although the general principles described in the previous paragraphs remain unaltered, certain modifications have recently been introduced. The following should be noted:—

i) Firstly, it is now specifically provided (Section 68 F.A.1976) that any expenses incurred in the provision of medical insurance (such as BUPA) are to be taxable on the employee concerned, even though he or she clearly cannot obtain any cash payment in respect of the insurance cost borne by the employer.

ii) It is now provided (Sections 36 and 37 F.A. (No. 2) 1975 and Section 71 F.A.1976) that certain *voucher* payments are to be taxable. Thus if an employee receives a voucher which he or she can exchange for goods or services, or indeed money, that voucher will now be taxable on the employee to the extent of the expense incurred in providing the voucher.

If no voucher which can be exchanged for goods or services is given, the general legal principles outlined in the preceding paragraphs apply.

Example

a)   Freda Worsnip has an agreement with her firm that they will pay for her to have a "free" hairdo once a month. This costs the firm £10 each time.

Since no voucher has been given by the employer, and Freda obviously cannot convert her hairdo into cash, this payment by her employer will not be taxable on her as a benefit in kind.

b)   Rita Chevrolet's employer gives her a £10 voucher to spend at the same hairdresser. Although according to the general legal principles of Schedule E this would not normally be taxable, it now unfortunately comes within the scope of the new provision concerning voucher payments. Since it costs the employer £10 to give her the voucher, Rita will be taxable on the sum of £10 under Schedule E.

PART II — PROBLEMS OF DIRECTORS AND HIGHER PAID STAFF

Introduction

If the principles enunciated above applied to all directors and senior executives, the situation might arise where say highly-paid company chairmen decided to take a modest cash salary but also had the company provide them with two free company cars (non-taxable because no cash conversion value), the use of a company yacht (non-taxable because no cash conversion value), 12 free suits a year (taxable only on their secondhand resale value) and so on.

To obviate this, the Inland Revenue has introduced rules which provide for a more penal basis of taxation on company directors and what may be termed "executives". The detailed rules, and their taxation consequences, are described in Chapter 4, but here an explanation will be given of the category of Schedule E taxpayer to whom these rules apply.

Persons to whom these rules apply

These are as follows:

i) Any company director, *regardless of his emolument level* (but see "Further Comments" below)

and ii) any Schedule E taxpayer whose total emoluments are £5,000 per annum or more (but see "Further Comments" below)

Anyone falling within this category of Schedule E taxpayer will find his benefits in kind taxed in accordance with the rules set out in Chapter 4, *not* in accordance with the rules explained in Part I of this chapter.

Further Comments

Although the general rule is that the more penal benefit in kind regulations apply to all directors and to employees whose emoluments exceed £5,000 per annum, there are some important qualifications and elaborations. The following should be particularly noted:

i) The Inland Revenue appears to take the view that all directors should come under this category, regardless of whether or not their emoluments exceed £5,000 per annum, because they are normally in a position to influence how their emoluments are paid. The Inland Revenue therefore seems to consider that such directors only take benefits in kind as opposed to cash because it suits their personal tax position to do so, and therefore anti-avoidance rules should be used to counteract this practice; but see point (ii).

ii)   The legislation provides (Section 69 (5) F.A.1976) that a director will not be regarded as a "director" for the purposes of the benefit in kind rules if he is not "interested" in more than 5% of the share capital of the company and is *either* a *f*ulltime working director of the company *or* works for a company which is non-profit making or charitable.

Any director fulfilling these conditions will therefore only be taxable if his total emoluments exceed the limits specified; that is to say, he will not be taxable because of the mere fact of his holding a directorship, but only if his emoluments are such as to bring him into the higher-paid range.

iii)   The term "emoluments" does not refer solely to cash payments. If it did, it would be all too easy for a senior executive (*not* director) to be paid say £4,999 in cash, and then to receive massive benefits which have no cash conversion value, such as company cars, company yachts and so on.

One must therefore proceed on the assumption that the employee *would* be liable to the more penal benefit in kind rules applicable to this category of Schedule E taxpayer, and to ascertain the value of his benefits in kind on that assumption. The taxable value of the benefits in kind will then be added to the actual cash receipts (see also point (iv) below), and if the resulting total is £5,000 or more, the provisions of Chapter 4 will apply. If the total is less than £5,000, the benefits in kind will be taxable in accordance with the principles outlined in Part I of this chapter.

iv)   In determining the level of "emoluments" all expense payments etc. made available by the employer must be included. For example, if an employee earns £3,900 a year and receives a company car worth say £400, he will clearly be below the £5,000 threshold figure. However, if he also incurs £900 worth of expenses which the employer pays, then EVEN THOUGH THE

EMPLOYEE MAY BE ABLE TO CLAIM THE WHOLE AMOUNT
OF THE PAYMENT AS AN EXPENSE RELIEF, his *emoluments*
will be in excess of £5,000 and he will be subject to the more
penal benefit in kind rules.

In Chapter 2 it was explained that "dispensations" could be
obtained from local Inspectors of Taxes whereby certain expense
payments, which represent a reasonable reimbursement by the
employer of genuine business expenses, are not considered as
income for Schedule E purposes and are not included on form
P11D at the end of each fiscal year. Where a dispensation in
respect of expenses has been received, the expenses included in
that dispensation (not other expenses) need not be counted for
the purposes of establishing the emolument level.

It is therefore important that wherever possible an employer
should agree a generous level of dispensations with the local
Inspector, to ensure that employees who are paid a modest salary
are not "artificially" brought within the special benefit in kind
rules merely by virtue of incurring substantial expenses (albeit
non-taxable expenses) during the course of the fiscal year.

v) The rules apply to emoluments paid *at the rate of* £5,000 a year
or more. Consequently, an employee paid at say £600 a month
who leaves the employer's service after 3 months is obviously
being paid *at a rate* exceeding £5,000 a year and will be subject
to the provisions of Chapter 4.

vi) In the 1977 Finance Act it was provided that the level of £5,000
would be raised to £7,500 as of 6th April 1978. This will result
in many executives being taken outside the benefit in kind net in
the 1978/79 fiscal year.

vii) It is specifically provided that where an employee has several
different employments with the same company or with the same
group (i.e. companies under common control) then *all* emoluments from these associated employments must be aggregated to
determine whether the threshold limit is breached. Were it not for
this provision, it would be all too easy to avoid the new benefit
in kind rules by the artificial fragmentation of employments
throughout a company or a group of companies.

Definition

From the foregoing it will be seen that all directors (with minor exceptions) and all employees whose emoluments exceed the threshold limit are subject to the provisions set out in Chapter 4 of this book. For ease of reference, the phrase "executive" will be used hereafter to denote a Schedule E taxpayer subject to the more penal benefit in kind rules (i.e. a person referred to in Section 69 (1) F.A.1976 as being a director or higher paid employee). This distinction will be maintained throughout the rest of the book and is of particular importance in Chapters 4, 5, 6 and 8.

CHAPTER 4

THE NEW FRINGE BENEFIT RULES FOR EXECUTIVES

This chapter itemises and explains the new benefit in kind rules applicable to "executives" (see the final paragraph of Part II of Chapter 3 for a definition of this term as used in this book).

The rules in this area were fundamentally recast by the 1976 Finance Act and subsequently modified by the 1977 Finance Act. For some years there have been special rules designed to tax benefits in kind for executives more heavily than employees generally but the old rules were swept away by the 1976 Act and a completely new set substituted.

The subject can conveniently be split into two main parts as follows:

PART I — REASON FOR THE CHANGE IN LAW

PART II — AN EXPLANATION OF FINANCE ACTS 1976/77

PART I — REASON FOR THE CHANGE IN LAW

The old rules taxing benefits in kind given to executives were to be found in Sections 195 — 203 T.A.1970.

Although these old rules initially seemed so wide in their scope that they applied to almost all conceivable benefits in kind, a closer examination of the legislation revealed a number of loopholes. For example:

i) The legislation only applied where the employer incurred some cost in the provision of a benefit for the executive. If no cost was incurred then there was no taxation consequence, *even though* a benefit may have been made available to the executive in question. One therefore always had to consider what the benefit had cost the employer, rather than by how much the executive had benefited. Indeed, a situation could arise in which the executive did not regard himself as having benefited at all, yet there was nevertheless a *taxable* benefit on him since the employer had incurred a cost. Typical examples of this type of benefit were the provision of interest free loans — unless of course the employer had incurred an identifiable cost in borrowing the money initially — and free air tickets given to airline staff.

ii) Secondly, the legislation only applied where the benefit was provided by the employer. It was possible for certain benefits in kind to be provided by someone who was not the employer as defined for tax purposes, and as a consequence these benefits were entirely free of income tax.

iii) The old rules were framed solely to tax benefits in kind provided for executives working for trading or investment concerns. Employees who worked for trade unions, charities or indeed for Government departments (such as the Inland Revenue!) were potentially not taxable on benefits in kind.

iv) As far as company cars were concerned, the benefit in kind assessable to tax depended on the amount of genuine business use made of the car, as compared with private use. In practice, however, the benefit of a company car often received lenient tax treatment.

For these and other reasons the old legislation was swept away. A completely new set of rules was introduced by Sections 60 — 72 Finance Act 1976. The majority of these new provisions came into effect as of 6th April 1977, although certain aspects (e.g. preferential loans; see Chapter 8) are as yet not effective.

PART II — AN EXPLANATION OF FINANCE ACTS 1976/77

Introduction

The new benefit in kind rules will be listed section by section below, accompanied where appropriate with a brief commentary

However, certain sections (e.g. those dealing with company cars) merit a chapter or part of a chapter in their own right. Where this is so, the section will be listed but the reader will be directed to the appropriate chapter in the book.

Before analysing the individual sections, two important points should be made:

i)   As explained in Part II of Chapter 3, the new benefit in kind provisions apply to *any* executive taxable under Schedule E. Thus, in contrast with the old benefit in kind rules, the new set make any Government or trade union officials or charity workers taxable in the same way as executives working for investment or trading concerns.

ii) The 1976 Act specifically provides that the new regulations apply wherever a benefit can be shown to be provided "by reason of the employment".

This phrase is important and should be contrasted with the old legislation, which stated that a benefit had to be provided by the *employer* to be taxable. Under F.A.1976, if the Revenue can show a connection between the provision of a benefit and a person's particular employment, then that benefit will be taxable as a benefit in kind, even though the provider of the benefit may have been a third party.

The Act also states that *any* benefit in kind made available by the employer is regarded as having been made "by reason of the employment". In the past some Schedule E taxpayers escaped tax liability on certain payments by their employer as it was held that the payment was not made because the person was an employee but for some other reason. This argument would appear to be no longer valid, and with the exception of certain benefits provided by *individual* (as opposed to corporate) employers which can be justified by virtue of some family connection, all benefits provided or made available by the employer are now deemed to be "by reason of the employment".

Throughout this chapter, and indeed in subsequent chapters, examples have been given of how the 1976 Finance Act rules operate, and suggestions put forward as to possible methods of alleviating their impact. For the sake of simplicity it has generally been assumed that the relevant benefit in kind is made available by the employer, but readers should always bear in mind that the provision of any benefit by third parties can be taxed in the same way *if* the Revenue can show that the benefit is made available only "by reason of the employment".

Section 60 F.A.1976

This section relates to payments by way of expenses, and provides that where any expenses are paid by reason of the employment to an executive — including any sums put at the executive's disposal and paid away by him — which would not otherwise be chargeable to income tax, then such expenses are regarded as emoluments of the employment and are accordingly chargeable to income tax under Schedule E.

Section 60 is therefore designed to catch for example lump sum expense payments which are sometimes made to executives. Of course, the fact that an expense may initially be taxable under Section 60 in no way precludes the executive from arguing at the end of the tax year that all or a proportion of the expenses have been incurred for genuine business purposes, and in this case relief in respect of these payments will be available.

When the Finance Act first appeared, some concern was expressed that this section may seek to tax the reimbursement of genuine expenses.

Example

Michael Byrne of Allied Shamrock Bank travels on business to Manchester and incurs out-of-pocket expenses (e.g. taxis, hotel bills etc.) of £100. On his return he seeks reimbursement from his employer.

In these circumstances, the employer would normally have sought a dispensation from the local Inspector of Taxes for the reimbursement of genuine reasonable business expenses. Therefore the employer could quite safely reimburse Michael with £100 gross without worrying about the possibility of deducting income tax as an emolument on the reimbursed payment in accordance with Section 60.

However, expenses paid or made available which are not subject to a dispensation agreement will be subject to the operation of Section 60, and will normally incur a deduction of income tax at the executive's appropriate rate on payment. However the executive will be able to claim relief at the end of the tax year if the expenses are for genuine business purposes.

Section 61 F.A.1976

This section introduces the general charge to taxation on benefits in kind.

The section states that where by reason of the employment a benefit in kind is provided for the executive *or* members of his household or family then that benefit in kind is potentially taxable on him. The actual amount of tax depends upon what is termed the "cash equivalent" of the relevant benefit; this term is defined in Section 63 of the Act (see below).

The scope of Section 61 is extremely wide in that it applies to "accommodation (other than living accommodation), entertainment, domestic or other services, and other benefits and facilities of whatsoever nature (whether or not similar to any of those mentioned . . . . ,)".

The wording of this section is extremely comprehensive. Some commentators have suggested that payments of *cash* (as opposed to benefits) cannot come within the scope of Section 61 because they are not specifically listed. The wiser view is however that all "benefits", including cash, fall within Section 61.

Section 61 is the general section applying to benefits in kind, but it is expressly held *not* to apply to specific benefits which come within the scope of other sections. Such benefits are considered to be of special importance and are each given their own section outlining the tax treatment in respect of them. Section 61 therefore excludes the following:

a)   Company cars (taxable under Section 64)

b)   Pooled cars (taxable under Section 65)

c)   Beneficial loan arrangements (taxable under Section 66)

d)   Employee shareholdings (taxable under Section 67)

e)   Medical insurance (taxable under Section 68)

As already explained, Section 63 specifies the taxable value for different benefits in kind covered by Section 61. It is important to appreciate therefore that Section 63 *cannot* apply in determining the taxable value of benefits falling within Sections 64 to 68 inclusive, since by definition such benefits do not come within the scope of Section 61, and therefore Section 63 does not apply to them.

Section 62 F.A.1976

This section elaborates on Section 61:

i)   Where a car is used insubstantially for business, it is stated that the provision of such a car comes within the scope of the benefits dealt with by Section 61 and *not* Section 64, which deals with company cars generally. This distinction is explained in detail in Chapter 6.

ii) The provision of a chauffeur for private (as opposed to business) use is also stated to come within the scope of Section 61, regardless of the fact that the chauffeur may be employed driving a car used "insubstantially" for business (Section 62), a business car (Section 64) or a pooled car (Section 65).

iii) Section 61 is stated not to apply to any accommodation, supplies or services occupied by the employer and made use of by the executive solely in performing the duties of his employment. Were it not for this exemption it could conceivably be argued that the provision of secretarial services, company notepaper and so on was a taxable benefit in kind!

iv) Chapter 2 described the new regulations dealing with rent free accommodation introduced by Section 33 of the Finance Act 1977.

Section 62 has therefore been amended to ensure that, where living accommodation is provided for an executive, any alterations or additions of a structural nature and any major repairs to the premises do not rank as benefits within the scope of Section 61.

v) It is specifically provided that Section 61 does not apply to the provision of pensions, annuities, lump sums, gratuities or other similar benefits payable on the executive's death or retirement.

This does not automatically mean that any form of pension or death-in-service provision made for an executive or his family is outside the scope of taxation. The reason for the exclusion here is because such costs are already taxable under the 1970 Finance Act and were it not for the exclusion contained in Section 62 the executive would potentially be taxable twice on the same benefit.

vi) Benefits consisting of meals in the employer's canteen are outside the scope of Section 61 *provided* the meals are available for staff generally. This matter is discussed in more detail in Chapter 5.

Section 63

This section seeks to specify in detail the cash equivalent of a benefit in kind, since in accordance with Section 61 above the cash equivalent represents the amount on which Schedule E income tax is levied.

The cash equivalent is the "cost" of the particular benefit minus any contribution made by the executive. For example, if the cost is £500 and the executive reimburses £200, the cash equivalent for taxation purposes will be £300.

The "cost" of any particular benefit depends on the type of benefit involved and thus can be any one of the following:—

i) If there is a clearly identifiable expense — for example if the company pays the executive's school fees — then the cost is the actual expense incurred.

ii)   If the benefit instead consists of an asset transferred into the
      executive's ownership, and this asset has been used or has depre-
      ciated in value, then the cost is regarded as the *market value* of
      the asset at the date of transfer. An example of this is shown in
      Chapter 5.

iii) Where the benefit consists of an asset placed at the executive's
      disposal, but without the legal title being transferred to him, then
      the cost is regarded as a combination of two factors: the "annual
      value" of the use of the asset, plus the total of any expenses
      incurred in or in connection with the provision of the asset.

     The definition of "annual value" itself depends on the asset under
consideration:

a)   In the case of land, the annual value is ascertained in accordance
     with Section 531 T.A.1970, which broadly means the rateable
     value of the land in question.

b)   In the case of a motorcar used insubstantially for business, the
     annual value is 20% of the original market value if the car is not
     more than 4 years old, and 10% if otherwise.

c)   In the case of all other assets, the annual value is 10% of the
     market value of the asset in question at the time when it is first
     used for benefit in kind purposes.

     The only exception to the above rules for determining annual value
relates to the renting or hiring of assets. Briefly, if the renting or hiring
charge paid by the employer exceeds the annual value determined under
(a), (b) or (c) above, then the renting or hiring charge will be used as
the tax basis instead. However, if the renting or hiring charge is *less*
than the annual value determined above, the renting or hiring charge
will be ignored and the annual value figure specified will stand. It is
therefore a case of heads the Inland Revenue wins and tails the taxpayer
loses! At one stage it was thought possible that the Inland Revenue
could include both the hiring charge and the annual value in determining
the taxable value of the benefit in kind, but recently the Inland Revenue

has issued a statement denying any intention of pursuing this point, although it appears on a strict interpretation of the legislation that they could do so.

Examples of the effect of the definition of cash equivalent are given in Chapter 5. The important points to emphasise here are:—

i)   If an asset is made available to the executive, the annual value and what may be termed the "running costs" of the asset must be added together to arrive at the cost of the benefit.

ii) Where the benefit consists of an asset being made available to the executive then the full annual value only applies if the asset is available for the entire fiscal year. If it is only available for part of the year, an appropriate fraction of the annual value should be taken. The same is true for the "running costs".

Section 63A F.A.1976

The detailed tax position regarding accommodation made available by an employer was dealt with in Chapter 2. Completely new rules relating to this subject were introduced in Section 33 of the 1977 Finance Act, and since the benefit in kind provisions dealing with accommodation apply to all employees, irrespective of status or salary level, there is no need to bring accommodation of this nature within the scope of Finance Act 1976 (as amended) applying only to executives. This particular section was introduced by Section 34 of the 1977 Finance Act, but with reference to the 1976 rules. Hence it is properly referred to as "Section 63A of the 1976 Finance Act", even though it was actually introduced one year later.

In Chapter 2 it was explained that in three specified situations,

i)   "proper performance" of the employee's duties,

ii) "better performance" of the employee's duties,

and iii) special threat to security,

a person is not taxable on the benefit of rent free accommodation provided by the employer. Section 63A goes on to state that, in the case of an executive chargeable in accordance with the provisions of the 1976 Act, he will only be taxable in a modified form on certain expenditure associated with the accommodation.

The expenditure involved is:—

a)   heating, lighting or cleaning the premises.

b)   repairs to the premises, their maintenance or decoration.

c)   the provision of furniture or other effects which are normal for domestic occupation.

Section 63A therefore provides that the employee cannot be taxable on expenditure by the employer on the above items on more than 10% of his net emoluments during the year. If the accommodation is only available for part of the year, then the 10% maximum is calculated by reference to a corresponding proportion of the year's emoluments. In essence, the executive's net emoluments are his earnings from his office or employment less any capital allowances deductible for tax purposes and less any contributions to approved pensions schemes.

Example

Michael Mellersh is a legal executive in a Government department working in a sensitive security area. Threats have already been made on his life and for this reason he has been provided with Government accommodation.

His income is £15,000 per annum and during the relevant fiscal year the Government pays:

a)   Heating and lighting bills totalling £1,000

b)   Decorators' bills totalling £500

c)   Furniture bills totalling £20,000

Under Section 63A Michael cannot be taxable on more than 10% of his net emoluments for the year — that is to say, £1,500 — in respect of the benefits specified.

Section 64 F.A.1976

This section deals with company cars used for business and is explained in detail in Chapter 6.

Section 65 F.A.1976

This section deals with "pooled" cars: that is to say, cars used by a number of executives as part of a general car pool. It is also explained in detail in Chapter 6.

Section 66 F.A.1976

This section deals with what are termed beneficial loan arrangements and is designed to levy a tax charge if either:

a)   A loan is made at a nil or low rate of interest,

or b)   if a loan is written off.

This subject is discussed in Chapter 8.

Section 67 F.A.1976

This section deals with the taxation of certain shareholdings owned by executives, and is explained in detail in Chapter 7.

Section 68 F.A.1976

This section deals with the taxation of medical insurance payments and does not refer solely to executives. All employees, whatever their status or emolument level, come within its scope. This section was explained in Part I of Chapter 3.

Section 69 F.A.1976

This section explains precisely which categories of Schedule E taxpayer come within the scope of the new benefit in kind rules. It was explained in Part II of Chapter 3.

Section 70 F.A.1976

This section provides for certain "dispensations", to obviate the need to submit details of routine expense payments and benefits which would clearly involve no extra tax liability.

If the employer explains to his local Inspector of Taxes his arrangements for paying expenses and for providing particular types of benefit, and satisfies him that in all cases such outgoings would be fully covered by an expenses deduction, the Inspector may give a dispensation. That is to say, he may notify the employer that, provided the circumstances remain unaltered, such payments need not be the subject of any official return and would not be included on form P11D for the executives in question.

Dispensations are usually given for payments of travelling and subsistence expenses, on an approved scale, for business journeys in the UK. They are not normally given for "round sum" expense allowances, nor for the entertaining expenses of employees of trading concerns.

Although an Inspector may have agreed a certain level of dispensation, he can always revoke it in writing; from then on income tax becomes chargeable and all returns must be made as if the dispensation was not in force.

Section 71 F.A.1976

This section deals with cash vouchers, which have been explained in Part I of Chapter 3.

Section 72 F.A.1976

This is an interpretation section which defines many of the terms used in the foregoing sections. For example:

i)   The term "director" is extended to include any person in accordance with whose directions or instructions the directors of a company are accustomed to act, even though that person may not be called a "director".

ii) The "market value" of an asset is the price which it might reasonably have been expected to fetch on the open market.

iii) Members of a person's family or household are his spouse, his sons and daughters and their spouses, his parents and his servants, dependants and guests.

Taxable Benefits in Kind

The main reason for the substantial growth in benefits in kind given to executives must surely be the UK's high marginal tax rates on income. Where taxable income exceeds £21,000, the tax rate is 83% and the executive is left with a mere 17p from each £1 of gross earnings.

Chapter 5 puts forward some suggestions as to how the benefit in kind tax rules can be ameliorated. However, even where an executive will be taxable on a benefit in kind, it is usually more efficient in terms of overall tax charge to give a benefit than a salary increase.

Assume that an executive wishes to acquire a benefit which will cost £170. To enable him to secure that benefit at his top marginal tax rate (83%), the company must give him a £1,000 gross increment. The executive will lose £830 in tax, leaving only £170 net. As far as the company is concerned, it would normally obtain corporation tax relief on the £1,000 salary payment, but even after relief at 52% it will still cost them in real terms £480 to give the executive a rise of £1,000 gross.

Therefore the executive will pay over £830 in tax to the Inland Revenue, and the true cost to the company will be £480.

If instead the company provided the executive with a benefit in kind, the position would be radically different. The executive would be taxable on the cost of £170, which even at his high tax rate would only mean a tax bill of just over £140. The company would obtain tax relief on the payment of £170, which means a true cost to it of some £82.

To summarise: the executive's tax bill is just over £140 (compared to £830) and the company's net cost is some £82 (compared to £480). The executive is of course £140 worse off in the sense that he must pay tax to this amount and has not received a salary rise to compensate. But the total saving in cost and taxation is substantial, and if the £140 tax loss to the executive can be made up in some other tax efficient way, the provision of a benefit in kind in this way undoubtedly seems preferable to the giving of a comparable salary rise.

CHAPTER 5

THE FRINGE BENEFITS THAT CAN NOW BE GIVEN

On the evidence of the previous chapter explaining the new benefit in kind regulations for executives, it may be wondered whether *any* such benefits can now be given on an advantageous tax basis. The scope of the legislation seems so all-embracing as to render tax planning a complete waste of time.

Nevertheless, although the situation is admittedly difficult, there is some opportunity for the inventive mind to make recommendations which may be helpful. Some ideas of this kind are contained in later chapters, i.e. those dealing with company cars, overseas emoluments and capital incentives. This chapter will therefore deal with a few ideas not covered elsewhere.

Most companies are aware that the real cost of an executive is much greater than his mere salary. When such expenditure as company cars, entertaining, company pension schemes, BUPA arrangements, national insurance contributions and so on are included, the total cost to the company is considerably increased. Many employers are now considering the introduction of what has been termed the "cafeteria", or *à la carte*, approach to emolument packages, whereby the executive can to some extent choose how his emoluments are made up — subject of course to the proviso that the emolument package does not exceed the present cost to the company of the executive. Depending upon individual circumstances and the tax efficiency of particular benefits in kind, two executives of similar status may have totally different emolument packages. While this approach is generally well received by executives, and certainly gives them more flexibility, employers should never lose sight of the fact that a "cafeteria" approach to remuneration packages may lead to problems, such as the following:

a)   If too many different types of benefit are available, the employer may find that the system becomes unwieldy and expensive from an administrative point of view.

b)   Unless the system is fully explained to staff, it may lead to jealousy. To take an extreme example: two executives of the same status may both "cost" the company £15,000 per annum. One executive may take his full £15,000 in salary, with no benefits in kind, whereas the other may take a company Rolls Royce, a company yacht and a salary of £1,000 a year. Unless it is clearly understood that the second executive is sacrificing substantial salary entitlements, it may be thought that he is receiving benefits dramatically in excess of those given to his counterparts.

c)   Difficulties may be experienced if a particular benefit in kind is applicable to staff generally and the benefits accruing from it are then increased. For example, this might arise in relation to pension scheme entitlement. One particular executive may decide, perhaps in view of his age and the absence of family commitments, that he wishes to forego favourable entitlement under the company pension scheme and elect for more tangible benefits such as company cars. Conversely, an executive nearing retirement age, with family obligations, would probably want the best available pensions deal, in preference to other benefits.

      The difficulty arises if the company should decide as a matter of policy to improve the general level of benefits under its pension scheme. As a result, the younger single executive will automatically receive an up-grading in benefits, but it will be difficult for the company to take away or reduce the value of his car. Thus the older executive is to some extent at a disadvantage in these circumstances, and this can lead to unrest.

Some examples of potentially tax-efficient benefits for executives will now be given. They are in no particular order, and no undue weight should be placed on any of the suggestions. Owing to the pressure of space, only brief details have been given, and companies wishing to implement any of the ideas should go into the matter further before doing so. Other tax advantageous benefits in kind, such as company cars, are dealt with in subsequent chapters.

1.   Cost to Employer

As explained in Chapter 4, the quantum of a benefit is quite often the cost to the employer, or to any other person providing the benefit by reason of the employment. As a simple illustration, if a company decides to pay for the school fees of an executive and these fees add up to £2,000, the *cost* to the employer (£2,000) will be regarded as a benefit in kind taxable on the executive concerned.

It follows that if the employer incurs no *cost*, then there can be nothing on which taxation can be ascertained, even though in the particular circumstances the executive may properly be described as having derived a "benefit". This situation may arise in many cases; the principle involved can perhaps best be illustrated by considering the tax position of an executive who works for British Airways.

Example

Charles Concorde is an executive with British Airways. He is quite keen to go to New York, and one morning he is told by the airline that there are some spare seats on the jumbo jet leaving at 10.30 a.m. Charles decides to accept this offer of a free seat and takes the flight.

Clearly, Charles has received a very valuable benefit, but is it taxable? To answer this question we must look at the cost of that seat to his employer. It would be too simplistic to consider the price for which the seat could be sold to the general public, since this is *not* the determination of taxable liability. We must ask ourselves "What has it cost British Airways to provide this seat"? The answer is of course *nothing*, since the aircraft would be leaving for New York at 10.30 a.m. anyway, and the fact that Charles is or is not on the plane makes no difference in practical terms. The cost to the employer is nil, and therefore the taxable benefit in kind levied on Charles is nil.

Doubtless, readers will be able to think of similar circumstances, particularly in the service industries, where the executive may receive a very worthwhile benefit but at no identifiable cost to the employer for the purposes of taxation.

2.   Goods Transferred by the Employer to the Executive

It was explained in Chapter 4 that where the legal title to an asset is passed from the company to the executive, the occasion of such transfer may lead to a tax charge.

Even though a tax charge may arise from the transfer, the effect may not be too disastrous if it is considered in relation to the overall financial benefits.

Example

> Mrs. Susan Cannings is the Chief Executive of NIT (National Industrial Training). She is a successful career woman paying tax at the marginal rate of 83% on the top slice of her income.
>
> Mrs. Cannings is very keen on hi-fi equipment and wishes to buy a music centre costing £340. At her tax rates she would have to earn £2,000 gross, leaving £340 net after 83% tax, in order to buy this equipment.
>
> What would happen if NIT first purchased the equipment, used it for say 6 months, and then passed it on to Mrs. Cannings? Most readers will be aware that hi-fi equipment is notorious for its rapid depreciation in value, and therefore after 6 months the second-hand retail value of the equipment may only be £100. If the equipment is then transferred to her, she will only be taxable on this market value of £100. At her tax rates, this means that she will only pay some £83 in income tax, which is obviously a dramatic improvement on the tax position if she had attempted to buy the equipment out of her pre-tax income.

Clearly, this principle of transferring an asset when its market price is substantially below its price when new can apply to numerous assets and may be used with advantage.

3.   Dining Facilities

The increasing cost of living nowadays means that the provision of executives with cheap or free meals becomes more and more attractive.

The author knows of several companies who provide such good lunch-time facilities that the executives now eat only one main meal a day. This serves to reduce the housekeeping paid to the spouse, which of course comes from the taxpayer's net spendable income.

It has been explained that dining ("canteen"!) facilities provided by the employer are not affected by the new benefit in kind rules, on condition that meals are provided for employees generally and not solely for executives.

Although no taxation problems have yet been experienced where some form of physical separation has been made between say the company directors and other employees, it has been suggested that such a separation may enable the Inland Revenue — on a strict interpretation of the law — to tax those meals given to executives as benefits in kind. Perhaps the safest course of action would be to provide one large dining area, but with areas of it partitioned off.

Although dining facilities provided by the employer on his premises are tax free, it must be stressed that any meal allowance given to executives (or employees generally for that matter) for the purposes of wining and dining outside will be taxable as part of the ordinary emoluments to the extent of the cash allowances given. The only modification to this rule relates to luncheon vouchers: provided the luncheon voucher is not transferable *and* can only be exchanged for food, the first 15p per day of luncheon vouchers given will be tax free. Although 15p per day towards luncheon does not sound very much, the benefit to the executive taxable at a marginal rate of 83% is almost £1 on gross salary.

4.   Staff Outings

Special occasions such as staff outings, annual dinner dances and so on are not in practice taxable on any recipient.

5.   Annual Value of the Use of Assets

As explained in Chapter 4, where an asset is made available to the executive, an "annual value" is attributed to the use thereof during the tax year.

With the exception of company cars (see Chapter 6) and land (see below), the annual value is generally taken as 10% of the *market value* of the asset at the time when it is *first applied* in the provision of benefits in kind.

Two points must be made here. Firstly, where an asset is about to be made available to an executive (or executives), it may be sensible for the company to make use of the asset first, in the hope of writing down its market value. This will mean that the executive is taxable on the reduced market value as opposed to the original market value.

Secondly, the "annual value" may be a quite favourable basis of taxation in circumstances where it can be coupled with the transfer of the asset at a subsequent date (as explained above in relation to hi-fi equipment). An example will explain this point more fully:

Example

Messrs. Sue Grabbit and Runne - - that well-known firm of leading London solicitors — feel that some of their managers are not dressing in a manner which befits their calling, and a memorandum is issued asking staff to each buy a decent suit.

John Writ, their litigation manager, is paying tax at a marginal rate of 83%, and tells the partners that a good suit costing £200 would cost him over £1,000 in gross salary. Is there anything the partners can do about it?

The partners decide to institute a "rent-a-suit" scheme. That is to say, the partnership itself buys a suit which it makes available to John Writ from time to time. This suit costs £200; therefore, as seen in the previous chapter, John will be taxable initially on 10% of the market value. His potential burden at the outset is therefore income tax at 83% on an annual value of £20. However, John is unlikely to wear the same suit every day of the year, but perhaps only one day a week. This immediately cuts the taxable figure for annual value down from £20 to say £3 a year.

After a couple of years, during which John has paid tax at 83% on an annual value of £3, the firm decides to transfer the suit to him as a gift. However, by this time the value of the suit is only £10, and thus John will be taxable in that year on a £10 gift — which will cost him £8.30 in tax.

This method therefore means that John has only paid tax on a total of £16, which even at his tax rate cannot be regarded as exorbitant!

6.   Annual Value of Assets used for only Part of a Year

Following on from the previous point, an employer may own a valuable asset, such as a company yacht or aeroplane, which an individual executive would be hard-pressed to afford. The ability to use this asset on an irregular basis must be considered a very valuable benefit when one bears in mind that, depending on the duration of use, the executive will only be taxable on a small percentage of the annual value − the percentage of 365 days represented by the actual period of use.

Example

Derek Dainton and John Mayhew, two executives of IETC (International Electrical Trading Corporation), both wish to spend a week cruising in the South of France. IETC has a boat, the present *market value* of which is £20,000 and which has not previously been used for the provision of benefits in kind.

The annual value of the use of the boat is initially 10% of the market value, that is to say, £2,000 per annum. Since Derek and John will be using the boat for just 1 week each, they will only be taxable on 1/52 of this figure − somewhat less than £40. Of course, any running costs etc. incurred during that week must be added, and become taxable as a benefit in kind. However, this does emphasise the fact that even where the use of an asset is taxable, in certain situations the tax charge may be quite acceptable. To be taxable, even at 83%, on a value of £40 for the use of a luxury yacht is somewhat lower than the typical open market value!

7.   Benefit to Employer and not to Executive

The new benefit in kind regulations are designed to tax benefits provided for the executive, his family and household, and not benefits provided to the employer for the employer's own use.

Employers should therefore realise that in some circumstances they may plausibly argue that it is they, the employer, who is benefiting and not the executive, or at least that any benefit derived by the executive is somewhat remote. If this argument is accepted, the executive incurs no taxation liability, since he has not received the benefit as such.

A good illustration of this is the situation regarding the provision of an in-house company doctor, dental facilities, etc.

Clearly, if the company incurred direct medical expenses (including BUPA) for an executive then this cost would be taxable, in accordance with the ordinary principles described earlier. However, what is the position if the company has a resident doctor or dentist available to staff generally? Has the company received a "benefit" by having a more contented and fit staff, and can the cost of this in-house facility ever be apportioned amongst executives?

Provided the facilities are available to staff generally, and are not confined to those of a certain status, the practical answer to the first question appears to be "yes", and to the second one, "no". Of course, the position would be quite different if the facilities were only available to say the Chairman and the Managing Director!

8.   Rent Free Accommodation

The detailed position regarding accommodation was discussed in Chapter 2, where it was noted that although specific exemptions from taxation have been granted to certain categories of taxpayer, it is normally difficult for an executive to bring himself within one of the exempt categories.

Even so, all is not lost, and in certain cases accommodation can be provided for an executive on a quite tax advantageous basis.

From a superficial inspection of the benefit in kind rules, it might be thought that rent free accommodation provided by the employer is taxable on the executive by reference to the open market rent which could have been received from letting the property in question on an arms length basis. This is not so, since the technical definition of annual value for land and property contained in Section 531 T.A.1970 states that the annual value is the *rateable value* of the property and not the open market rental value. For the purposes of this discussion, it is assumed that the property has been purchased by the employer and made available to the executive. Different considerations apply if the property is leased; see Chapter 2 for further particulars.

Example

Tax Mitigation Services Limited wish to provide their Chairman with a rent free London *pied à terre*. The Chairman normally lives in Neasden but sometimes needs to stay in London, either because he is meeting overseas customers or because he wishes to frequent Fifi's Go-Go Rave Bar in the heart of Mayfair.

The rateable value of the property is £500, but the open market rent which could be obtained on an arms length basis is £4,000 per annum. Since it is the rateable value which determines the taxation liability, the Chairman will only be taxable on a benefit in kind of £500 per annum, not £4,000 per annum.

Of course, the Chairman will presumably not make use of the *pied à terre* on every day of the fiscal year; he may on average use it 2 days a week. This being the case, he will be taxable on 2/7ths of £500, which is rather less than £150 per annum.

To this annual value must be added appropriate running costs.

As mentioned above, Chapter 2 also explains in detail the new regulations applicable to company housing introduced by the 1977 Finance Act.

9.   Benefits for "Working" Wives

It has been explained that the provision of benefits in kind to an executive's spouse, family or members of his household will be taxable in the same way as if the benefit had been made available to the executive himself. Consequently, there initially seems to be no taxation advantage in providing benefits in this way; although it is a moot point whether a mistress comes within the definition of a member of one's household or family!

Nevertheless, advantages may be obtained if the benefits in kind are available to a working wife, who works in the business and who is not regarded as an executive for the purposes of the benefit in kind rules. One tends to find husbands and wives working together in either:

     a)   Large companies, such as banks and insurance companies, where the husband and wife often meet on the staff,

or b)   Small companies; it is quite usual in a family business for the wife to assist her husband with bookkeeping, secretarial work and similar office duties.

If the employer is able to provide the spouse with a lower level of emoluments, with benefits in kind which have a low or nil cash convertible value (as was explained in Chapter 3), such benefits may be extremely tax efficient, whereas their efficiency will be much less if given to a spouse regarded as an executive for taxation purposes.

A question frequently asked is to what extent the Inland Revenue may contend that the provision of benefits in kind for the "working wife" is really no more than a device to minimise the overall family taxation burden. Provided matters are arranged correctly, this contention can be rebuffed. The two areas demanding particular attention are:—

i)   In the case of a family business, the possibility of the Inland Revenue arguing that the wife is in reality a "director" of the company. If this argument succeeds then, as explained in Chapter 4, the benefits would be taxable in accordance with the new regulations, even though the emolument level might be less than the specified minimum (£5,000—£7,500 per annum).

ii)   Whether the benefit given to the wife is in reality a benefit which the employer regards as belonging to the husband. An example will illustrate this point:

Example

     Mr. and Mrs. Benefit work for the Home Help Insurance

Company in London. He earns £10,000 per annum and she earns £4,000 a year.

The insurance company decides to give Mrs. Benefit a company car. Since she is not an executive for the purposes of the more penal benefit in kind rules, the benefit of this car should entirely escape taxation liability. However, had the car been made available to Mr. Benefit, the car would have been taxable in accordance with the principles explained in Chapter 6.

The real test is whether Mrs. Benefit would keep the car if for some reason Mr. Benefit left the insurance company's service. If she did retain the car for use, it would appear that the Inland Revenue's contention is weak. However, if Mrs. Benefit forfeited the use of the car on Mr. Benefit's leaving the company's service, the Revenue would have a very strong case for saying that in reality the car was provided for Mr. Benefit and should thus be taxable on him, even though it was notionally made available to his wife.

10. Expense Claims Generally

Executives nowadays tend to ensure that they claim every out-of-pocket expense incurred in connection with performing their duties, and which can thus be reimbursed by the employer tax free. In the past, few people would have bothered to claim small items such as taxi fares, minor entertainment and so on, but now the position has completely changed.

Similarly, claims are increasingly being made in respect of the "business use" of home telephones, professional magazines and indeed newspapers. The author knows of one case where an executive allegedly made a successful tax claim for buying the *Daily Mirror* each day of the week!

11. Travelling Expenses

The only expenses deductible in calculating Schedule E liability are those which can properly be shown to be "wholly, exclusively and necessarily" incurred in the performance of the respective duties. The difficulty of obtaining allowable deductions for Schedule E expenditure has been explained previously in this book.

The attitude of the Inland Revenue is that, since an executive's duties cannot commence until he is actually at work, the expenses involved in travelling from home to the place of work and back are not incurred for the purposes of *performing* these duties. This should be compared with the position in Germany, for example, where certain expenses of commuting are tax deductible.

Although the cost of travelling to and from work can present problems for Schedule E purposes, the following possibilities may be considered:—

i)   In certain cases an employer may now be able to pay for all private motoring in respect of a company car. This is explained in the next chapter.

ii)   A number of companies have been persuaded to run coaches, at the employer's expense, to the place of work. Even though such coach facilities have been used in part by staff regarded as executives, such people have never in practice been taxable on the value of the benefit of free coach travelling. Indeed, it may be argued that the benefit accrues to the company, in the sense of enabling them to keep all the staff working for them, rather than to the individuals who travel by the coach.

iii) By concession the Inland Revenue regard an employee of a "group" as having one base at which he is employed, and consequently any travel between group members or group offices is regarded as being wholly, exclusively and necessarily incurred in the performance of the duties.

      It may therefore be sensible for a group with offices all over the country to employ its senior members of staff at the company nearest to that person's home, even though the executive may normally work for an office or company in the group some distance away. Thus, although the cost of travelling from home to the office will not be deductible for tax purposes, it is possible to minimise this outgoing, since once the executive has established a *base* then any travelling on from that base is, by concession, allowed. To what extent this technique can be used obviously depends on the particular circumstances of the case.

Summary

Although the above list does not claim to be exhaustive, it does perhaps give a reasonable indication of the areas in which a creative employer can provide tax efficient benefits in kind for executives. Other benefits worthy of consideration are considered in subsequent chapters.

As far as possible, employers should make available those benefits in kind which do not cause excessive administrative work.

CHAPTER 6

TAXATION OF COMPANY CARS IN DEPTH

Introduction

As explained in Chapter 4, the 1976 Finance Act fundamentally changed the taxation of benefits in kind made available to executives. One of the more important of these changes related to the taxation of company cars.

This chapter will therefore analyse the new rules on company cars as they apply to executives. The basic position regarding benefits in kind for employees was discussed in Chapter 3, where it was seen that generally speaking a company car made available to an employee who is not an executive will be entirely free of personal taxation, even though that car may be used mainly for private as opposed to business purposes.

The subject of executive cars can be broken down into several main headings. Until one has established under which heading the particular car comes, it is not possible to determine accurately the taxation consequences. In this chapter the cars will be analysed according to the following classification:

1. Cars with little or no business use.

2. Business cars which are available for private use.

3. Pooled cars.

4. Cars owned by the executives themselves.

The term 'car' is specifically defined (in Section 72 (5) F.A.1976) as 'any mechanically propelled road vehicle except —

i)   a vehicle of a construction primarily suited for the conveyance of goods or burden of any description,

ii) a vehicle of a type not commonly used as a private vehicle and unsuitable to be so used,

iii) a motorcycle as defined in Section 190 (4) of the Road Traffic Act 1972, and

iv) an invalid carriage as defined in Section 190 (5) of that Act . . . .

It has for example been held that a driving school car is of a type which falls within section (ii) of this definition; see the case of Bourne v. Auto School of Motoring (Norwich) Limited (1964).

1.   Cars with little or no business use (Ss. 62 and 63 F.A.1976)

A car comes within this category *either* if it is not used at all for business travel *or* if the business travel is 'insubstantial' compared to the private use made of the car during the tax year. Therefore the use of a car on a year-to-year basis will determine whether that car comes under this heading, or − preferably, from the taxpayer's point of view − under the 'business car' heading considered next.

Unfortunately the word ''insubstantial' is not defined in the legislation, and presumably the Courts will ultimately have to decide whether, in their judgement, a car has been used insubstantially for business purposes. In the eyes of the Inland Revenue, a car is used insubstantially for business if the amount of business use does not exceed 10% of the total use during the tax year. This was confirmed in an Inland Revenue press release of 11th November 1976, which went on to say that, in this context, special attention would be given to cases where:

a) Two or more cars were provided for the use of the executive (or his family),

or b) where a car appeared to have been provided more in recognition of the executive's status than in recognition of his job and the business use this involved.

Wherever possible it is important to avoid a car being classified as a non-business car, since the taxation in respect thereof will invariably be higher than for a business car (see below).

The taxation charge for a non-business car is calculated as follows:—

> i) The executive will be taxable on 20% of the market value of the car when new (or 10% of the market value of the car when new if the car is more than 4 years old)

plus ii) all running costs, petrol costs, insurance costs. road fund tax and similar payments.

Example

John Director has 2 company cars. One is a Scimitar — which he uses for business purposes and which the Revenue accept as a business car — and the other is a 'runabout' made available to his wife. The runabout is a brand-new car and cost the company £2,000. During the tax year the company pays running costs of £400.

As far as the wife's car is concerned, John Director will be taxable on £800 per annum as a benefit in kind: that is to say, the £400 running costs plus 20% of the cost of the car when new (i.e. 20% of £2,000). This sum of £800 will be added to his otherwise taxable emoluments and income tax levied accordingly.

The following points should be noted:—

a) The tax charge is reduced by the extent to which the employee contributes towards the cost of the benefit. For example, if John Director pays £300 to his company in return for their making available — and paying for — the car to his wife, the taxable benefit in kind will be reduced from £800 to £500.

b) Even though the car may be used insubstantially for business purposes, there may be some element of business use during the fiscal year. If so, this genuine business use will not be taxable, since the intention of the legislation is to levy a tax charge on private as opposed to business benefits. Any genuine business use will therefore serve to reduce the taxable value of the car.

c)   As explained in Chapter 4, where an asset is hired or leased by a
       company and the hiring or leasing payment exceeds the 'annual
       value', the tax charge can be based on the hiring payment. Con-
       sequently, in the above example, if the company paid £500 to
       hire the 'runabout', the £500 cost would be substituted for the
       annual value figure of £400. However, had the car been hired at a
       cost of only £300, then the annual value figure of £400 would
       have remained the taxable base.

2.   Business cars which are available for private use (S. 64 F.A.1976)

Attention must now be turned to the business car covered by Section
64 of the 1976 Finance Act: that is to say, the company car which the
executive (or his family, etc.) can use for private purposes. The phrase
'private use' denotes any use of the car made by the executive and
members of his family or household otherwise than for business travel.
       Most readers will doubtless be aware that the legislation (Schedule 7,
F.A.1976) specifies a table of rates of taxable benefit in respect of
different categories of car. The tables are as follows:—

TABLES OF FLAT RATE CASH EQUIVALENTS

Table A

Cars with Original Market Value up to £6,000
and having a Cylinder Capacity

Cylinder capacity of car in cubic centimetres	Age of car at end of relevant year of assessment	
	Under 4 Yrs	4 Yrs or more
1,300 or less	£175	£120
More than 1,300 but not more than 1,800	£225	£150
More than 1,800	£350	£235

Table B

Cars with Original Market Value up to £6,000
and not having a Cylinder Capacity

Original Market value of car	Age of car at end of relevant year of assessment	
	Under 4 Yrs	4 Yrs or more
Less than £2,000	£175	£120
£2,000 or more but less than £3,000	£225	£150
£3,000 or more but not more than £6,000	£350	£235

Table C

Cars with Original Market Value more than £6,000

Original Market value of car	Age of car at end of relevant year of assessment	
	Under 4 Yrs	4 Yrs or more
More than £6,000 but not more than £10,000	£500	£335
More than £10,000	£800	£535

From the above it will be seen (Table A) that the taxable value of cars costing not more than £6,000 is determined partly by the age of the car and partly by its engine size, whereas for cars costing over £6,000 (Table C) the taxable value depends on the age of the car and its price. Table B may strike readers as a rather curious one, since it relates to cars which have no cylinder capacity! However, it should not be thought that the government is attempting to levy a tax charge on cars with no engines; as the more technically-minded will no doubt be aware the table is designed to cater for the rotary engine and the electrically-driven car.

Thus the executive will initially have the appropriate figure from the above tables added to his taxable income for the fiscal year in question. However, from this simple starting point, a number of additional considerations should be taken into account:

i)   If the car is not available for private use at all, then there will be no taxable benefit. The above tables only apply to a business car which is *available* for private use during the year.

A recent question in Parliament sought confirmation of the fact that, if an executive's Contract of Service stated that the car was not available for private use, then there was no benefit in kind on which he could be taxable. The government minister confirmed that this was the case, *provided* that no private use was made of the car as a *matter of fact*. Therefore, although a statement that the car is not available for private use may be helpful, this will not absolve the executive from a tax charge if the contract provisions do not accord with the true facts.

ii) The figures in the above tables are reduced if the car is unavailable to the executive for any part of the year. A car is regarded as being unavailable on a particular day if, as a matter of fact, it is not available — possibly because it is being used by someone else. Alternatively, a car is regarded as being unavailable if it is not possible to use it at all for a period of at least 30 consecutive days — a situation which might arise if a car is overseas or is undergoing extensive repairs.

Example

On 6th July the executive takes possession of a 3,000 c.c. car costing £5,500. He uses the car until September 5th, when he goes on holiday for a month. During this month the car is left at the office and is used by the executive's secretary. The executive returns to the office on October 6th and uses the car until December 21st, when he runs into a lamp-post driving home from the office party. The car is off the road being repaired until January 20th, and the executive then uses the car in the ordinary way until the end of the fiscal year (April 5th 1978).

From Table A, it will be seen that the ordinary taxable value of the car is £350, by virtue of its age, cost and engine c.c. However, the executive could not have had use of the car for the first 3 months of the fiscal year (April 6th to July 5th); furthermore, he was unable to use the car for a month while he was on holiday, and for a month while the car was off the road being repaired. He would therefore be taxable on only 7/12ths of £350 for the year 1977/78, a taxable benefit in kind of £204.

For convenience, this example has been worked out in whole months, although the legislation does provide for calculations on a day-by-day basis.

iii)   The figures set out in the tables may be reduced by 50% if the executive uses the car in question to drive at least 25,000 business miles per annum. If he drives 24,999 miles no relief will be given, but if he covers an extra mile or two then the scale charges on which tax is payable will be only half of those specified.

This figure is extremely high for genuine business mileage, and in various parliamentary debates attempts have been made to reduce it, so far without success.

In many ways it is illogical to make the 50% reduction dependent upon mileage rather than upon the percentage of total use. For example, a salesman covering Scotland *may* drive a total of 45,000 miles a year, of which 25,001 are business miles and the remainder constitute private use. A salesman covering the London area may only drive 12,000 miles during a year, but of this total possibly 10,000 miles could be genuine business miles. Although in *proportional* terms the London salesman has driven much more for business purposes than the Scottish salesman, the latter will have his taxable benefit in kind reduced by half, whereas the London salesman will be taxable on the full scale specified in the tables.

iv)   The charges specified in the tables may be reduced if the executive is required, as a condition of the car being made available for his private use, to pay an amount of money for that use. To take a simple example: if the managing director receives a brand new car costing the company £8,000, he will initially be taxable (by virtue of Table C) on £500 as a benefit in kind. If however he has to pay say £300 for the right to have that car available for private use, the taxable charge on him will be reduced to £200.

Two points should be emphasised here. Firstly, the payment must be made as a condition of the car being available for his private use. If it is for any other reason it would seem that the reduction in the taxable value will not be allowed.

Secondly, the payment must be made for 'that *use*'. The only safe way of ensuring that this condition is fulfilled is for the executive to make a flat payment for the use, with no further strings attached. Some companies have apparently experienced difficulties in cases where the executive has agreed to pay say the road fund licence and/or the car insurance; it has been argued that the payment he has made is not for the *use* of the car as such, but for road fund licence, car insurance or whatever. Although local tax inspectors may not always take such a harsh view, it is recommended that fixed payments without further specification are made, to avoid this potential problem of disallowance.

v)   Earlier on in this chapter the difference between 'non-business' (S. 62/63) cars and 'business' (S. 64) cars was explained. Attention was also drawn to the Inland Revenue press release which stated that particular attention would be given, *inter alia*, to those executives with two or more company cars.

The mere fact of having two company cars does not automatically mean that one of them will always fall foul of the harsh benefit in kind taxation rules applicable to non-business cars. There may well be genuine business reasons for having two cars: for example, the managing director of a company may need a 'status' car when touring round company offices or entertaining overseas customers. However, if he has to come down to London frequently, it might be appropriate for him to have a small car which consumes less petrol, can be parked more easily and so on. On this basis a local Inspector of Taxes may well accept the argument that both cars fall within Section 64.

vi)   The taxable value of a car is determined partly by its original market value. The term 'original market value' does *not* mean the cash purchase price to the business

The original market value is defined as that applicable to the car at the date of its first registration, including where appropriate car tax but not VAT.

Example

Tax Avoiders Limited decide to buy a vintage Bentley for their Chairman. The present market value — and the cost to the company — of the car is £20,000, but the original price of the car when first registered many years ago was only £1,000.

In determining the taxable value of the car, one must consider the original market value of £1,000. The present-day cost to the company is quite irrelevant. In addition, since the car is by definition more than 4 years old, the reduced taxable benefits columns in Tables A, B and C above will apply! Similar rules apply to non-business cars covered by Section 62 and Section 63 Finance Act 1976.

vii)   Perhaps the most contentious aspect of company cars concerns the financing of private running costs. When discussing the non-business car, it was seen that private running costs are taxable as a benefit in kind, but this does not automatically apply to business cars.

The position appears to be that if the executive fills up his car with petrol, uses that petrol for private purposes and then seeks reimbursement from his employer, the Inland Revenue will regard this as a reimbursed expense falling within the provisions of

Section 60 F.A.1976 (explained in Chapter 4). Thus in these circumstances private petrol would be taxable in the ordinary way.

However, if the executive does not seek reimbursement of the expense, but throws the expense *at the outset* on to the shoulders of the employer, it would appear that the employer can finance all private petrol without the employee being taxable thereon. The ideal way of achieving this would be for the employer to open one or more garage accounts in the *employer's* name which the executive could make use of. All private petrol purchases would therefore be charged by the executive to the employer's garage account, and since there would be no *reimbursement* to the executive, the private petrol would not be taxable. The alternative way of achieving non-taxable private petrol paid for by the employer would be to use company credit cards. In much the same way, the employer would initially assume the responsibility for payment of the bill, and the executive would not claim any form of reimbursement. In this connection, employers should first ascertain which credit card companies are prepared to issue credit cards in this way for use by executives but with the obligation for payment falling solely on the employer.

The credit card method is not as watertight as the garage account method. Garage owners supplying petrol might consider the executive as the person responsible for paying the petrol bill, and may not be aware that the obligation for payment falls on his employing company. It has therefore been argued that this method might run into problems, since the employer may be said to be taking over a pecuniary liability of the executive; if this is so, then this will of course be taxable under the general rules applicable to Schedule E emoluments (explained in Chapter 2). In practice, however, it is understood that the Inland Revenue will accept company credit cards used in the way described as absolving the executive from tax liability. Credit cards would therefore appear to be an acceptable — and certainly more flexible — alternative to garage accounts.

Some employers may not wish to pay for their executives' private mileage. Even so, there is scope for tax planning if the employer is prepared to be accommodating. Let us assume that the executive has a car with a taxable value of £350. He may agree with his employer that he should pay £7 a week (say, £350 per annum) for the 'use' of that car. The employer may in turn be prepared to disburse that £7 per week in paying for the executive's private petrol.

Provided this is done correctly, the executive's tax burden on the company car will be nil, since the payment of £350 will cancel out the benefit in kind valuation of £350, and the executive will have £350 of private petrol financed tax free. This technique might also be useful for pay code purposes, since it may serve to reduce the value of the 'benefit' of a company car to nil.

3.   Pooled Cars (S. 65 F.A.1976)

Anyone who is not prepared to pay tax in accordance with the business car rules described above may attempt to argue that their car is a 'pooled' car for the purposes of Section 65 F.A.1976. If the executive can successfully claim that his car comes within this definition it will be entirely tax free and Tables A, B and C set out above will not be relevant.

To fulfil the conditions of Section 65, the executive must 'satisfy' the local tax inspector that during the fiscal year in question his car has been included in a car pool. Much depends on the amenability of the inspector, and on the skill of the executive, the company and their taxation advisers in proving that a particular car is a pool car. Little is so far known about how inspectors will interpret the legislation, and of course individual inspectors might adopt different attitudes.

Before the Inspector of Taxes will accept that a car is a pool car, three conditions must be fulfilled. To meet one or two of the conditions is not sufficient; all three must be complied with. These conditions are:

a)   Firstly, the car must be available to, *and be actually used by*, at least two employees, and no one employee may use the car 'ordinarily' to the exclusion of the other or others.

Clearly this is a question of fact, and these facts will usually be known only to the employer or executives and not to the Inspector of Taxes. Furthermore, the other people who use the car may be employees whose emoluments are below the point where the more penal taxation on benefits in kind applies (see Chapter 3).

b)   Secondly, any private use made by the executive must be merely incidental to the business use made of the car.

The word 'incidental' has not been statutorily defined and may eventually be subject to judicial scrutiny. It has been confirmed, however, that travelling between home and the office can properly be described as use 'incidental' to business use.

c)   Thirdly, the car must not normally be kept overnight in, or in the vicinity of, any residential premises where any of the employees is residing — although the car may be kept overnight on premises occupied by the employer.

This is perhaps the hardest condition to meet, since most executives will wish to garage the car at home. Again, phrases like 'in the vicinity of' are as yet undefined and a commonsense approach must be adopted. It has been suggested that one method of avoiding the problems posed by this third condition would be for the executive to sell or lease his garage to his employer. The car would then indeed be garaged in the *employer's* premises, which is permissible, and not the executive's premises, which is forbidden.

Any individual executive using a car which he feels ought to be treated as a pooled car may make a claim to this effect to the Inspector of Taxes. Alternatively, the employer may make an application in respect of the car for all the executives concerned. If the inspector does not accept that the car is a pooled car, the matter may be appealed to the Commissioners or to the Court. Once a determination has been made by the Commissioners or the Court, that determination is binding on all the executives concerned, not just the one actually involved in the proceedings.

Furthermore, once a particular car has been determined upon, that determination cannot be appealed against in respect of the same car in the same tax year. Thus, if a company owns car "A", which has been turned down for pooled car treatment in say June 1977, that car cannot be subject to a further appeal for such treatment until 6th April 1978 at the earliest. It would therefore be advantageous to the employer or executives to dispose of car "A" and acquire car "B", since car "B" can be appealed against in the 1977/78 year.

4.   Cars Owned by the Executives Themselves

Lastly, an executive may buy his own car and use it for business purposes. This course of action is initially attractive, for the following reasons:—

i)   Firstly, the executive may be able to claim income tax relief on any loan raised to buy his 'company car' (see Paragraph 12, Schedule 9, F.A.1972). This entitlement may be claimed for at least three full fiscal years.

ii)   Alternatively, the employer may be able to lend the executive money to buy the car on an interest-free basis, without the absence of interest being regarded as a taxable emolument within the scope of Section 66 F.A.1976 (the subject of interest-free loans is dealt with in Chapter 8).

iii)   The executive will be able to claim, within the usual limit, capital allowances for income tax purposes to write off the cost of the car's depreciation.

        Under present legislation, the maximum allowance per annum is £1,250. Therefore the executive is potentially able to write off up to this amount of the cost of the car each year for income tax purposes. If the car is used only partly for business, then the amount written off must of course reflect this fact.

        If the employer has made an advance to the executive to help him buy his car, then, as explained in Chapter 8, the writing-off of this loan in whole or in part will normally lead to an income tax charge in the year in question. If, however, the executive is able to claim capital allowances as described in the previous paragraph, then the writing-off of the loan may be matched by the deductible capital allowances in such a way that they cancel each other out and thus not lead to any tax charge.

iv)   The executive may be allowed to deduct all business mileage 'wholly exclusively and necessarily' incurred, or alternatively he may seek reimbursement from the employer on some agreed basis.

Some employers wish to pay their executives an agreed rate per mile where the executive uses his or her own car. This payment will reflect not only the direct costs, such as petrol, but also indirect costs, such as overheads, depreciation, road fund licence, insurance, etc. The amount of this mileage allowance which a company can reasonably reimburse to the executive must depend largely on the opinion of the local Inspector of Taxes, which will vary from area to area. For example, the Inland Revenue feels that the reimbursed mileage rate can be somewhat higher in London, where wear and tear and petrol use are greater, than in say Scotland, where there is less traffic and less congestion, leading to longer engine life, more economical petrol consumption and less wear and tear generally.

The Revenue will probably accept a mileage rate reimbursement of about 8p a mile for a car under 1,000 c.c., 9–10p a mile for a car between 1,000 and 1,800 c.c., and 11–12p a mile for a car over 1,800 c.c.. It must be stressed, however, that these are only very approximate guidelines, and that everything depends on the rate which can be agreed with the employer's local Inspector of Taxes. Rates substantially in excess of the above can sometimes be agreed in particular cases.

Where an Inspector of Taxes agrees a mileage rate on the basis outlined, such a rate will usually be the subject of a dispensation which will mean that, as explained earlier in this book, the payments are not subject to P11D treatment; furthermore, they will not be taken into account when determining whether the recipient is an 'executive' and thus more heavily taxable on benefits in kind.

Whether it is more attractive for an executive to own his own car, as explained in this section, or to have a business car falling within Section 64 provided by his employer is a matter of debate, but generally speaking the fewer business miles the employee does each year, the more beneficial it will be for him to have a business car provided by his employer rather than to own and run his own car.

Provision of Chauffeur

The provision of a company chauffeur is an expense totally distinct from the provision of a company car of any of the types described in this chapter. Consequently, any executive who has available to him a chauffeur for *private* as opposed to business use will be taxable on that benefit according to the general rules of Section 62 F.A.1976. A just proportion of the cost of the chauffeur to the company will be taxable on the executive (or executives), dependent upon the private use made of the company chauffeur.

Future Legislation

It is difficult to foretell the course of future legislation in this area. To a large extent it must depend on the politics of the government in power.

Most executives, one imagines, will be in the position of having a business car taxable under Section 64 in accordance with Tables A, B and C, and it is not inconceivable that in future years the Inland Revenue may seek to modify the regulations in respect of private petrol payments. As far as the actual rates set out in Tables A, B and C are concerned, they may be amended by statutory instrument from 6th April 1978 onwards.

Perhaps the most interesting aspect will be the way in which the provisions applicable to pooled cars are interpreted in practice. This of course is the provision from which government ministers are exempt in respect of the use of Ministry cars.

CHAPTER 7

EXECUTIVE SHARE OPTION AND INCENTIVE SCHEMES

As explained in Chapter 2, where a Schedule E taxpayer receives a valuable right to acquire shares as part and parcel of his remuneration, the value of that entitlement will be regarded as an emolument and taxable in accordance with the principles of Schedule E.

Generally, however, executives are invited to take up share options or special classes of share in their employing company in circumstances where the "acquisition" is not a taxable emolument. Special rules have therefore been framed to deal with the taxation of such schemes, and those rules are described in this chapter.

The legislation in this area is of exceptional complexity, and in a chapter of this length the author can only discuss some of the main principles and perhaps highlight some of the potential pitfalls. During the last decade the tax rules have been changed on several occasions, the most recent being in the 1976 Finance Act.

The subject will be dealt with under the following headings:

PART I   – RECENT HISTORY

PART II – SHARE OPTION SCHEMES

PART III – SHARE INCENTIVE SCHEMES

PART IV – FINANCE ACT 1976

PART I – RECENT HISTORY

The most logical point at which to commence a discussion of executive share schemes is the 1972 Finance Act. This Act provided that if a share option or incentive scheme complied with certain conditions laid down by the Inland Revenue, then that scheme was "approvable" by the Revenue for taxation purposes, in much the same way as a pension scheme.

The effect of Inland Revenue approval was that:

i)   No tax liability would accrue when the executive entered the scheme.

ii) . No tax liability would accrue when the executive actually acquired the shares, e.g. by converting the option, by paying up partly paid shares, or whatever.

iii) A *capital gains tax* liability would only arise when the shares in question were finally disposed of.

At the same time as introducing these beneficial rules of approval, the Inland Revenue also devised numerous anti-avoidance provisions which meant that the tax legislation would radically affect schemes which did not comply.

The 1974 Finance Act swept away, with substantial retrospective effect, the possibility of a share scheme being approved for tax purposes. The present intention of the law is clearly to impose an *income tax charge* whenever an executive makes a capital profit in circumstances where it can be said he acquired shares "by reason of his employment". The Labour government claimed that it was not hostile to executive share schemes but merely wished to ensure that the profits made were "correctly" classified as income profits, not capital profits!

Although the 1974 Finance Act removed the possibility of obtaining Inland Revenue approval for share schemes, it unfortunately left all the anti-avoidance rules intact. Thus companies and their advisers are left with the worst of both worlds, and expert advice is now needed before establishing any such scheme.

As mentioned above, the 1976 Finance Act has introduced further potential tax penalties on executive incentive schemes, but *not* on share option schemes.

PART II — SHARE OPTION SCHEMES

Introduction

Share option schemes have traditionally been the most popular method of giving executives some form of capital stake in their employing company. Share options are very simple to operate: the option is granted to the executive in return for a modest payment and entitles him to acquire shares in his employing company at today's price. If the shares rise in value it will profit the executive to exercise his option and acquire the shares. Conversely, if the shares fall in price the executive need not buy the shares and can merely allow his option to lapse.

The option is normally valid for a specified period, usually between 3 and 7 years.

Tax Liability

Whenever the option is exercised and shares are acquired, there will be a deemed income tax profit equal to the difference between the open market price of the shares and the amount given for them. Alternatively, if the taxpayer decides to assign his option right, and thus receives in return a similar sum, an income tax charge will likewise arise on this disposal.

The legislation applicable to share option schemes is mainly contained in Section 186 T.A.1970, but this has been supplemented by Section 77 F.A.1972. The effect of this latter enactment is to create further difficulties where the share option is capable of lasting for more than 7 years and the shares can be acquired at less than their market value.

Some examples will serve to illustrate the taxation problems involved:

Example

Section 186 T.A.1970 applies to *any* Schedule E taxpayer, whether or not an executive, who realises a gain from a share option scheme obtained by virtue of being a Schedule E taxpayer. Consider the case, therefore, of Mark Smith and Ken Jones, two executives of A.B. Common Limited who are both paying tax at a marginal rate of 50%.

1. Mark Smith pays £1 for the right to acquire 100 Common Ltd shares. He may acquire these shares for £1 each, and their present market price is £1.50. The option can be exercised at any time during the next 6 years.

   After 4 years, when the shares have risen in value to £6 each, he takes up his option and buys the shares.

   Mark will therefore be taxable as follows:—

		£
Market value of shares when option exercised (£6 x 100)		600
Less price paid by Mark:		
Cost of option	£1	
Cost of shares	£100	101
Income taxable profit		£499

   Mark will therefore have to pay tax on £499 at 50%, which equals £249.50.

2. Ken Jones has a similar entitlement to Mark, except that his option can be exercised over a 10-year period.

   His tax liability is therefore as follows:—

Year 1		£
Market value of shares to be acquired (100 shares at £1.50 each)		150
Less: Amount payable on exercise of option	£100	
Cost of option	£1	101
		£49

   Ken Jones will therefore incur an *immediate* income tax charge on a deemed profit of £49, and by virtue of S.77 F.A. 1972 his tax bill in year 1 will be £24.50.

Year 4		£
Market value of shares on conversion of option		600

Less:	Cost of option	£1	
	Cost of shares	£100	
	Amount already taxed	£49	150

£450

Thus in year 4 Ken Jones will pay a further income tax charge on this £450 profit, which at a 50% tax rate means a bill of £225.

Therefore, both Mark Smith and Ken Jones have paid the same overall amount of tax, but Ken paid part of his tax at the time the option was granted, whereas Mark paid all his tax when he exercised the option.

Further Tax Considerations

1. If either Ken or Mark dispose of their shares subsequently, they will normally pay capital gains tax on the increase in price. For example, if Mark sells the shares acquired from the option 5 years later for £2,000, he will pay capital gains tax at the maximum rate of 30% on the deemed profit of £1,400 (i.e. £2,000 minus £600).

2. In certain circumstances, particularly when the shares acquired under the option are in some way restricted, those shares can be regarded as "incentive" shares subject to the rules described in Part III below. If this is so — and it must be stressed that this situation seldom occurs — then any capital profits made on realisation of the shares themselves would also be liable to income tax!

3. The above examples assume that both Mark and Ken pay tax at 50%, but the addition in one fiscal year of a large capital amount

which is regarded for taxation purposes as income may push the executive up through several tax bands to the top rate of 83%.

Example

Sir Herbert Surtax is the non-executive chairman of Rubber Plant Enterprises. His taxable emoluments for 1977/78 are £6,000 and thus his income is fully taxable at the basic rate of only 34%.

Sir Herbert realises a gain of £25,000 under the company's share option scheme, which means that for the fiscal year his income has risen from £6,000 to £31,000. Consequently, income tax at ever-increasing rates will be chargeable on different segments of the share option scheme profit, and the top £10,000 will be taxable at 83%.

It may be thought reasonable that where a profit has arisen over say 3 or 5 years only a proportion of the profit should be included in the taxpayer's income calculation for the year of realisation. This is true, for example, of the taxation of single premium life assurance policies, whereby the total profit is divided by the number of complete years over which the profit is regarded as having been made. In Sir Herbert's case, let us assume that the share option scheme had matured over a 5-year period. Therefore the "average" profit each year is £5,000. It would be more equitable to add this £5,000 to Sir Herbert's other taxable income of £6,000 for the purpose of establishing an appropriate tax rate or rates. These lower rates of income tax could then be applied to the total profit of £25,000.

Unfortunately, the Inland Revenue has not yet seen fit to give relief of this nature.

Revenue Return

Any employer granting a share option, or indeed allotting or transferring shares in pursuance of an option, is under a statutory obligation to advise the local Inspector of Taxes of that fact within 30 days of the end of the relevant fiscal year. Similar rules apply to share incentive schemes, described in Part III below.

Overseas Considerations

i)   The income tax charge described above will only arise if the employee is taxable under Schedule E Case I in the year in which the option is *granted*. Consequently, if an executive working overseas becomes entitled to a share option and subsequently returns to the UK, he may be able to convert the option into shares without falling foul of these tax rules, since at the time he was granted the option he was not liable to UK tax in accordance with Schedule E Case I.

ii) An executive may become entitled to a share option from his employer in circumstances where he is taxable in accordance with Schedule E Case I but is not in the UK during the fiscal year when the option is converted into shares.

Although there is a technical liability to income tax, as a *matter of practice* the Inland Revenue will not pursue the tax claim, *provided* the sole or main reason for leaving the UK during the fiscal year was not to avoid tax liability under the option scheme.

iii) If an option scheme is made available to UK employees but in respect of shares in an overseas company, the Bank of England must give consent. The difficulties are such that share schemes devised for executives in respect of overseas companies are usually of the "incentive" type described in Part III.

PART III — SHARE INCENTIVE SCHEMES

Introduction

An executive share incentive scheme usually takes the form of the acquisition by an executive of shares in his employing company, as opposed to *options* to buy shares. The shares are usually acquired by means of an interest free loan; alternatively, partly-paid shares can be made available, for which the executive initially pays say only 1p a share, and provides the balance of the subscription price after the expiry of a number of years, when it is hoped that the shares will have risen in price.

Legislation

The basic legislation dealing with share incentive schemes is Section 79 F.A.1972, which applies to the situation "Where a person acquires shares or an interest in shares in a body corporate in pursuance of a right conferred on him or opportunity offered to him as a director or employee of that or any other body corporate". This part of the chapter is therefore solely concerned with people who work for companies and who by virtue of their employment are given the right to buy shares in their employing company. It is not concerned with:

i)   Any Schedule E taxpayer who buys shares on the open market for their full value,

or ii)   anyone who acquires shares by virtue of his contract of employment and is thus taxable on the value of those shares as part of his emoluments. This situation was discussed in Chapter 2.

Effect of Legislation

Subject to certain exceptions (e.g. if the shares are acquired under a profit sharing scheme as part of taxable emoluments), the effect of Section 79 is to render liable to income tax under Schedule E any increase in the market value of incentive shares over a period beginning at the date when the shares are acquired and ending on the *earliest* of the following dates:—

i)   7 years from the date of acquisition

ii)   The date when the director or employee in question ceases beneficially to own the shares,

or iii)   the date on which "restrictions" are removed (see over).

In consequence, an income tax charge will arise in the fiscal year in question, in the same way as with share option schemes. Again, there is no measure of relief from higher tax rates, and the whole profit is regarded as income from the appropriate fiscal year, even though the profit may be fairly said to have arisen over several years of share ownership.

Example

> Jeffrey Brown of Haricot Verts & Co. joins the company share incentive scheme. He is given an interest free loan to acquire shares presently worth £1 each.
> After 7 years he still owns the shares and their value has risen to £5. Consequently, he will be taxable *then* on his deemed profit of £4 (£5 minus £1) per share, even though he has not yet disposed of the shares. The income tax charge falls on the *earliest* of the three events listed above, and such a charge can arise even though no capital profit has actually been made by the executive.

"Restrictions"

A share is subject to "restrictions" if there is some condition imposed — either by the company's Articles of Association or by some agreement, contract or arrangement — which in some way restricts the executive's freedom to dispose of the shares, or indeed to exercise rights conferred by the shares. Alternatively, any conditions which might mean that the disposal of shares or exercise of rights would result in some disadvantage to the person concerned are also regarded as restrictions: for example, the deposit of the shares as security for a loan made by the employer to finance the acquisition of the shares in the first place would be considered as a "restriction".

It would clearly be tempting to circumvent the share incentive scheme regulations by issuing shares subject to massive restrictions (e.g. no voting rights, no dividend rights and so on). While subject to these restrictions, the shares would have little or no value, but if and when the restrictions were lifted, the shares could become extremely valuable.

To stop the issuing of shares with artificial restrictions as a means of reducing the Schedule E income tax charge, the lifting of those restrictions has been made the occasion on which the income tax charge may accrue, provided of course the lifting of restrictions occurs prior to the disposal of the shares and/or to the expiry of 7 years after the date of their acquisition.

Overseas Aspects

1. Like the share option scheme rules, the scope of the share incentive scheme legislation is confined to Case I Schedule E taxpayers. It will therefore be a defence against the Inland Revenue to state that the shares were acquired while overseas.

2. If shares are acquired, but at the time the tax charge might arise the executive is overseas, then in the same way as with share option schemes, the Inland Revenue will not in practice pursue its claim for income tax, unless the sole or main reason for the executive's departure was to avoid income tax liability in the UK on the shares in question.

3. If the executive wishes to acquire incentive shares in an overseas employer, the Bank of England must be consulted. Before giving their approval, the Bank will require full particulars of the arrangement.

    One important condition for Bank of England approval is that the shares to be acquired overseas should be in a quoted company, or at least in a company whose shares will be quoted shortly. Taxpayers wishing to join share incentive schemes based on non-quoted overseas companies would probably not obtain approval from the Bank of England.

4. The new rules concerning overseas emoluments introduced by the Finance Act 1977 (and described in Chapter 9) may reduce the tax liability in respect of share incentive schemes.

    Chapter 9 explains that relief is now available in respect of duties performed wholly or *partly* outside the UK and, depending on the degree of absence, either 100% or 25% of the emoluments attributable to the overseas duties is free of tax.

Since capital profits made under a share incentive scheme are regarded as Schedule E income profits, and since the whole or part of one's income can be excluded from tax by virtue of overseas duties, then a similar proportion of the profits made under a share incentive scheme should be exempt from tax. This would appear to be so, even though at the date when the executive joined the incentive scheme he had no overseas duties, and such overseas duties only commenced in the same fiscal year during which the profit under the share incentive scheme was realised. A careful examination of the 1977 Finance Act rules on overseas duties is to be recommended.

PART IV — FINANCE ACT 1976

Introduction

New rules have been introduced, partly effective from 6th April 1978, to levy income tax under Schedule E on the benefit of what are termed "beneficial loan arrangements". These are loan arrangements where there is no obligation to pay interest, or only interest at a reduced rate. Furthermore, a Schedule E tax liability will arise if the loan is written off. Part II of Chapter 8 gives further details.

The effect of Section 67 F.A.1976 is to introduce the tax treatment of beneficial loan arrangements into the share scheme legislation. In consequence, the provisions briefly listed below are only relevant to executives, whereas the previous comments in this chapter have been applicable to Schedule E taxpayers generally. In practice, however, only "executives" are normally given the opportunity of joining share option and incentive schemes.

The special rules outlined in this part of the chapter only apply to share incentive arrangements and have no relevance to share option schemes.

Shares Acquired at an Under Value

Where shares are acquired at an under value, the executive will be regarded as having received an interest free loan of an amount equal to the "under value". Therefore the executive will be charged Schedule E tax each year on the amount of commercial interest which ought to have been paid on an arms length basis.

Shares are regarded as having been acquired at an under value if they are partly-paid shares or shares purchased by way of loan (i.e. the full purchase price will fall due some time in the future). In either case the income tax charge on the notional interest will apply each year until the full amount of the original market price of the shares is paid. However, since the provision which makes an income tax charge on the notional interest of beneficial loans does not take effect until 6th April 1978, the effect will not be felt until then.

Stop Loss Provisions

In addition to levying a tax charge on shares acquired at an under value, Section 67 of the 1976 Finance Act also imposes an income tax charge under Schedule E in respect of what are termed "stop loss" provisions.

The usual object of a stop loss provision is to ensure that where an executive has acquired under an incentive scheme shares which have fallen in value, he will suffer no loss. The shares might be bought back at their original value, or payment at the *current value* of the incentive shares may be accepted in satisfaction of any outstanding balance of the original purchase money due from the executive.

The beneficial loan arrangement provisions described in Part II of Chapter 8 also apply to this situation. Consequently, if an executive is protected against capital loss in this way it will be regarded as tantamount to the writing-off of a loan, which means that the executive will be taxable under Schedule E on the amount so written off. The executive will still be taxable even though he may have left the employment of the company before he benefits from the stop loss provision, and even though he may have suffered a salary reduction (to the extent that he is no longer an "executive" for the purposes of this book) by the time the stop loss provision operates.

The imposition of a Schedule E charge on stop loss protection takes effect from 6th April 1976. Only shares acquired after 6th April 1976 are affected, and consequently those acquired prior to that date continue to benefit from stop loss protection without the imposition of a tax charge.

Miscellaneous

The basic effect of Section 67 F.A.1976 has been described above, but the rules are so complex that they would repay careful study.
  For example:

i)   Section 67 applies to "shares" and, while this excludes share options, it does include stock, securities and all *interests* in shares.

ii) The rules extend not merely to shares acquired by the executive personally but to shares acquired by anyone "connected" with him, provided that their acquisition can be shown to be by reason of the executive's employment.

CHAPTER 8

GOLDEN HANDSHAKES
AND OTHER TAX EFFECTIVE CAPITAL PAYMENTS

With UK income tax rates at their present high level, it is clearly desirable for a Schedule E taxpayer to receive a payment which might be considered as *capital* rather than income. The maximum rate of tax for such a capital payment will normally be only 30%.

This subject will be considered under the following three headings:

PART I   – LUMP SUM PAYMENTS ON TERMINATION OF AN OFFICE OR EMPLOYMENT

PART II – "BENEFICIAL LOAN ARRANGEMENTS" – SECTION 66 F.A.1976

PART III – MISCELLANEOUS ITEMS

PART I – LUMP SUM PAYMENTS ON TERMINATION OF AN OFFICE OR EMPLOYMENT

Introduction

It is important to appreciate at the outset that there are two different types of such payment:

i)   *compensation* payments for loss of office,

and ii)   *ex gratia* payments made without legal obligation on the cessation of service.

Although both payments are taxable on roughly the same principles, there are detailed differences which will be explained later.

Corporation Tax Relief

Although this book is not concerned with the corporation tax aspects of particular payments or benefits, an exception must be made here, since generally speaking only payments properly regarded as being of a revenue nature are deductible for corporation tax, and capital payments are not deductible.

However, a lump sum paid to an employee on his leaving service is normally always deductible for corporation tax purposes; that is to say, the fact that it represents capital in the hands of the executive or employee does not prevent it from being a corporation tax deductible revenue expense for the employer. If the payment is genuinely *ex gratia* it is deductible for corporation tax on the basis that it engenders staff goodwill: the fact that the company has rewarded a particular employee who has left their service should make that company a more "attractive" employer to the remaining staff. Alternatively, where the payment is made as compensation for loss of office, its purpose is to free the company from what might be regarded as an onerous or inhibiting contract.

In both cases it can quite properly be claimed that the payment has been made wholly for the benefit of the trade or business of the employer.

Such payments will however not be deductible for corporation tax in the following circumstances:—

i) If the severance payment is made in the course of a liquidation, or as part of an arrangement for the discontinuation of trading. This situation arose in the case of Godden v. Wilson (1961), where it was established that when a company is in the process of terminating its trade or business, it cannot be argued that the payment was made for that trade or business.

ii) If the severance payments are negotiated as part of a take-over agreement, or as part of an agreement to alter the capital holding of one or more of a company's shareholders. The payments will in these cases be regarded as of a capital nature from the point of view of the company, rather than of a trading nature. This will mean that the payment is not corporation tax deductible.

General Taxation Provisions regarding Termination Payments

We must turn now to the general legal position of the Schedule E taxpayer who receives a payment on severance. The mere fact that a Schedule E taxpayer receives a lump sum on the termination of his office or employment does not of itself give that lump sum the nature of a capital payment or indeed remove it from the category of taxable emoluments. Liability to tax depends upon the *nature* and *purpose* of the payment. The fact that the payment is given a particular name by the parties to the arrangement is not conclusive, and the Courts will examine the true intention of the payment in order to ascertain whether it represents income or *capital* to the recipient.

Until 1960, where a sum was held to be a capital payment it entirely escaped taxation. However, in that year the Inland Revenue introduced what were popularly termed the "golden handshake" provisions, designed to levy an income tax charge in circumstances where the payment was technically a capital payment to the recipient. These provisions have now been consolidated into Sections 187 and 188 (and Schedule 8) T.A.1970, explained below.

The numerous judicial decisions concerning lump sum payments on severance give rise to some confusion, since many of them appear to conflict. However, the following basic principles seem to apply:

a)   Whenever there is a pre-arranged agreement, either in the contract of service or in the company's Articles of Association, which provides that a fixed sum will be paid on the cessation of the office or employment, this is regarded as a form of deferred emolument and fully taxable as earned income under Schedule E. There is *no question* of any part of the payment being tax free under the "golden handshake" rules described below; the full amount specified is taxable as Schedule E income in the appropriate year.

In the case of Henry v. Foster (1931), the company's Articles of Association provided for a payment of "compensation for loss of office" in the event of a person ceasing to be a director, provided he had served for at least 5 years. The director retired and sought to enforce payment. In the words of the judge: "The payment to the respondent, whatever the parties may have chosen to call it, was a payment which the company had *contracted* to make to him as part of his remuneration for his services as a director".

Likewise, in the case of Dale v. De Soissons (1950) the taxpayer made a service agreement providing that the company would pay him £10,000 as "compensation for loss of office". The judge held that the £10,000 was not compensation for loss of office as such but profits from an office or employment: "In the present case the taxpayer surrendered no rights. He got exactly what he was entitled to get under his contract of employment. Accordingly the payment in my judgement falls within the taxable class".

Thus it must be stressed at the outset that in order to mitigate taxation on severance payments, such payments must not be "contractual".

b)   Similarly, any payment made with regard to future services (e.g. for withholding resignation or for serving at a reduced salary) is regarded as an advance of remuneration and is thus fully taxable under Schedule E.

c)   On the other hand, any payment made *not* by virtue of a service agreement but as a consideration for release from or surrender of the employee's rights under a service agreement is not regarded as an emolument and thus prior to 1960 was entirely free of tax.

d)   The Inland Revenue may sometimes claim that where a compensation payment is made *before* the date of the termination which gives rise to it, then in reality it is an emolument of the employment. For this reason payment is not normally made until after the cessation of employment; the executive or employee might hand in his resignation in return for a post-dated cheque.

Provided the compensation payment is *immediately* connected with the termination of the taxpayer's service, there is normally no need to post-date the compensation cheque. The Inland Revenue will not query the payment simply because it was made slightly before the actual moment of termination. On the other hand, if the compensation payment is part of an arrangement whereby the executive or employee must continue in service for a period of weeks or months, then the Inland Revenue will almost certainly regard it as taxable remuneration rather than compensation for loss of office.

Section 187 T.A.1970

We have discussed the basic legal position, and that which applied prior to 1960. Now for the present-day situation.

Section 187 T.A.1970 is designed to levy tax on any payment made to a person on the occasion of his ceasing to hold an office or employment, where that payment would not otherwise be liable to income tax. For example, if a service contract provides for a specified lump sum to be paid on termination, this payment will be taxable as an ordinary Schedule E emolument and therefore the rules described below will not apply.

Section 187 is drafted in wide terms. For example:

i) The provisions apply even where the lump sum payment is not made by the employer but by some other person.

ii) The provisions apply where the payment is made not to the former executive or employee but to a spouse, a relation or a dependant of such person. Even payments made to a deceased Schedule E taxpayer's legal personal representatives can be taxed.

iii) Where some consideration other than cash is given, the value of the payment is regarded as the value of that consideration in money terms at the time it is given.

iv) All lump sum payments made under Section 187 must be notified to the local Inspector of Taxes by the employer soon after the end of the fiscal year during which payment is made.

Section 187 therefore provides that lump sum payments of the nature described are taxable, subject to any relief which may be appropriate in the circumstances. The relieving provisions are described below. Any payments taxable in accordance with Section 187 are classified for tax purposes as earned income, not investment income.

Section 188 T.A.1970

Section 188 grants relief in respect of certain payments which would otherwise be fully liable to Schedule E income tax in accordance with Section 187 above. The chief exemptions are:

i)   Payments made in connection with a termination resulting from the death, injury or disability of the employee.

ii) Any sum which has already been chargeable in accordance with the provisions of Section 34 T.A.1970; that is, certain payments made in consideration for entering into restrictive covenants.

iii) Benefits payable under approved retirement schemes.

iv) Certain payments to H.M. Forces.

v)   The first £5,000 of any payment chargeable under Section 187 (see below).

vi) Payments in connection with overseas employments and duties. This particular topic will be considered later.

The £5,000 Exemption

Sub-Section (3) of Section 188 provides that tax will not be charged in respect of any payment not exceeding £5,000, and where the payment does exceed £5,000 then income tax under Schedule E will be charged only on the excess.

Where two or more payments which are liable to tax are made to the same Schedule E taxpayer for the same office or employment — or indeed for different offices or employments held under the same employer or with associated companies — then all such payments must be aggregated in order to ascertain whether the £5,000 limit has been exceeded.

. Where payments are associated in this way, but are paid in different fiscal years, the £5,000 exemption is deducted from the payment regarded as income from the first period before it is deducted from income regarded as being from a later period. Subject to this, the £5,000 exemption is divided between the two payments in proportion to their respective amounts.

Example

Michael Dean has employment contracts with Bondi Beach Trading Limited and Rent-a-surfboard Limited. Rent-a-surfboard Limited is a wholly owned subsidiary of Bondi Beach Trading Limited.

Michael retires from Bondi Beach Trading Limited on 31st March 1977 and from Rent-a-surfboard Limited on 1st May 1977. He receives a "golden handshake" of £12,000 from the first company and £15,000 from the second, making a total of £27,000.

Since the payment of £12,000 from Bondi Beach Trading Limited is received in the fiscal year 1976/77 it is taxable in that year.

	£
Lump sum payment for 1976/77	12,000
Less: S.188 exemption	5,000
Taxable for 1976/77	7,000

The further payment of £15,000 would be taxable in 1977/78. Since the employments are "associated" the £5,000 exemption has already been used up, and therefore the £15,000 will be fully taxable in 1977/78, with no reductions.

Standard Capital Superannuation Benefit

Schedule 8 T.A.1970 also gives relief in respect of certain payments otherwise fully chargeable under Section 187 T.A.1970. The "standard capital superannuation benefit" relief should be particularly noted. This is designed to exempt payments *in excess of £5,000* to people who have worked for their employers for a long period of time. However, it must be emphasised that:

i)   The standard capital superannuation benefit relief cannot be claimed in addition to the £5,000 relief. Thus, if the standard capital superannuation benefit is £10,000, this would be granted in preference to the £5,000 reduction.

ii) The standard capital superannuation benefit relief car. only be claimed in respect of *ex gratia* payments. It is not available where the payment is a compensation for loss of office.

The standard capital superannuation benefit relief is calculated by reference to a complex formula:

$$\frac{N}{20} \times AE - L, \text{ where}$$

N   =   number of *complete* years of service

AE   =   average earnings during the 3 years prior to termination of employment

L   =   any tax free lump sum which may be taken from the company's pension scheme.

Example

Christopher Green has worked for the *Cambridge and Fleet Street Chronicle* for 40 years. His earnings in the 3 years before his retirement are £15,000, £20,000 and £25,000. He takes his entire pension scheme entitlement in the form of a pension, and not as a tax free lump sum (see Chapter 10).

Since Christopher's average earnings over the 3 years are £20,000 a year (£15,000, £20,000 and £25,000 divided by 3), the calculation is thus:

$$\frac{40}{20} \times £20,000 - 0$$

$$= 2 \times £20,000 - 0$$

$$= £40,000, \text{ the standard capital superannuation benefit}$$

Therefore Christopher may receive a "golden handshake" of up to £40,000 entirely free of tax.

If however he had decided to take £10,000 in tax free cash from the company pension scheme, this would have reduced his tax free entitlement from £40,000 to £30,000.

"Top Slicing" Relief

Despite the reliefs mentioned above, substantial income tax liability might arise if the total taxable value of the "golden handshake" were to be included in the taxable income for a single year. Since the "golden handshake" in fact represents income for several years, Schedule 8 T.A.1970 has introduced what is colloquially termed "top slicing" relief. The basic concept behind this is that the extra income tax attributable to the payment is to be calculated as though only a certain fraction of it, the "appropriate fraction", were chargeable in that fiscal year; the rate of tax is calculated by reference to this fraction, and that rate is then applied to the taxable gross amount of the "golden handshake".

Although the concept is simple, the actual calculation of this relief is very complicated, since it involves four computations:

i)   The income tax payable on the total income of the taxpayer including the taxable value of the "golden handshake" must first be ascertained, then   ii)   the tax payable on the total income *excluding* the "golden handshake" must be calculated,

then   iii)   the difference between (a) the income tax payable if only the "appropriate fraction" of the "golden handshake" is received,

and (b) the tax payable if no such fraction is received

must be ascertained; in both cases any emoluments received from the office or employment must be ignored.

The amount of relief is calculated by taking the result of computation (i), subtracting from it the result of computation (ii) plus the "appropriate multiple" (the inversion of the "appropriate fraction") of the difference calculated in (iii).

Example

David Cox and Bert Box both receive a "golden handshake" of £30,000 from their employers Break Up Insurance Brokers. In both cases only the first £5,000 is tax exempt under Section 188.

David Cox receives an income from his employment of £12,000 during the year prior to termination, but Bert Box only receives £3,000 during the year prior to termination. David Cox, acting on professional advice, does not take up any other employment for the remainder of the fiscal year during which the "golden handshake" was received. However, Bert Box does take another job, and during the tax year he receives total emoluments of £9,000 from this new job. David Cox has £2,000 of investment income and Bert Box £6,000 of investment income. They are both paying mortgage interest of £3,000 a year.

On the assumption that they each receive £2,000 of personal allowances, the relevant tax calculations are as follows: —

Tax Calculation 1 (Income tax payable on total income including taxable value of "golden handshake")

	David Cox	Bert Box
	£	£
Income from job	12,000	3,000
Investment income	2,000	6,000
Income from "new" job	–	9,000
	14,000	18,000
Plus: taxable value of "golden handshake" (first £5,000 exempt)	25,000	25,000
	39,000	43,000
Less: Mortgage interest £3,000 Personal allowances £2,000	5,000	5,000
Taxable Incomes	34,000	38,000
Approximate income tax liability	22,000	25,500

Tax Calculation 2 (Tax payable on income excluding "golden handshake" payment)

The £25,000 "golden handshake" payment is deducted from the above figures in both cases. Thus, Mr. Cox's income is reduced to £9,000, and Mr. Box's to £13,000. The income tax payable by Mr. Cox is approximately £3,400, and by Mr. Box about £5,800.

Tax Calculation 3 (Difference between tax payable if only the "appropriate multiple" of the golden handshake is included; in every case ignoring emoluments of the office or employment from which the payment arises).

(a)   The last step is to ascertain the difference between the tax payable if only the "appropriate fraction" of the golden handshake is received and that payable if no such fraction is received, ignoring *in both cases* any other emoluments from that office or employment. In the case of an *ex gratia* payment the "appropriate fraction" is 1/6, and the "appropriate multiple" is therefore 6 (6/1). If however the payment is compensation for loss of office, the appropriate fraction is 1 divided by the number of years of unexpired service. The "appropriate multiple" is of course the number of years of unexpired service. For example, if a taxpayer was dismissed with 8 years of unexpired service, the "appropriate fraction" would be 1/8 and the "appropriate multiple" would be 8.

We shall proceed on the assumption that the payments under consideration are *ex gratia*.

In both cases the taxable payment is £25,000. This is divided by 6 to ascertain the "appropriate fraction", which is therefore £4,167. Unfortunately Bert Box has taken another job during the tax year and this remuneration of £9,000 must therefore be included in the calculation:

	David Cox	Bert Box
	£	£
"Appropriate fraction" of golden handshake	4,167	4,167
Investment income	2,000	6,000
Plus: Income from *other employment*	–	9,000
	6,167	19,167

Less: deductions & reliefs	5,000	5,000
Taxable income	1,167	14,167
Approximate income tax payable	400	6,500

Tax Calculation 3b

The same calculation is repeated, this time ignoring the "appropriate fraction" of the golden handshake. Thus David Cox's income is reduced to £2,000 and Bert Box's to £15,000. Since they each have £5,000 worth of allowances, the allowances more than cover David's income, which is therefore nil for tax purposes. However, Bert Box has an income of £15,000, partly from his investment income and partly from his new employment, and even after deducting £5,000 of allowances, this taxable income is still £10,000. His tax burden is therefore approximately £4,000.

Tax Calculation 4

The "top slicing" tax relief can now be calculated. The tax liabilities from the four previous calculations can be summarised as follows:

	David Cox	Bert Box
	£	£
Calculation 1	22,000	25,500
Calculation 2	3,400	5,800
Calculation 3a	400	6,500
Calculation 3b	—	4,000

The relief is therefore the difference between Calculation 1 and Calculation 2 *plus* the "appropriate multiple" of the difference ascertained between Calculations 3a and 3b (in this case 6).

For David Cox, the "appropriate multiple" of the difference between Calculations 3a and 3b is £2,400 (i.e. £400 x 6). For Bert Box the figure is £15,000 (i.e. £2,500 x 6).

The relief for David Cox is therefore £22,000 − (£3,400 + £2,400) = £22,000 − £5,800 = £16,200.

The relief for Bert Box is therefore £25,500 − (£5,800 + £15,000) = £25,500 − £20,800 = £4,700.

Therefore, David Cox's relief is almost four times that given to Bert Box, even though their "golden handshakes" are of the same amount. The moral is that one should not take another job during the same fiscal year in which the "golden handshake" is received. Thus the "golden handshake" should be given as near to the end of the tax year as possible.

Overseas Employments

In certain cases where a person works for substantial periods of time overseas, the "golden handshake" applicable to the overseas service is entirely free of tax.

Furthermore, where a person is entitled to the 100% deduction in respect of foreign duties (described in Chapter 9), any "golden handshake" in respect of these duties is exempt from taxation. However, Schedule E taxpayers only entitled to the 25% deduction *cannot* claim any special relief (i.e. 25% of any "golden handshake" will *not* be considered tax free).

PART II − "BENEFICIAL LOAN ARRANGEMENTS"− SECTION 66 F.A.1976

Introduction

Prior to the Finance Act 1976, the benefit of a nil or low interest rate loan made available to an executive normally escaped income tax. The only exception was if the Inland Revenue could prove that the employer had incurred an identifiable expense in obtaining the loan, i.e. if he had borrowed the money to pass on to the executive interest free. In this case the executive would have been chargeable on an amount equal to the cost to the employer.

The tax position relating to what are termed "beneficial loan arrangements" has been modified in two respects by Section 66 F.A.1976:

1. **Absence of Interest**

If a loan is made to an executive, or members of his family or household, and either no interest or an uncommercial rate of interest is charged, the executive will normally be taxable on an amount equal to the commercial interest which ought to have been paid.

The income tax charge is levied by reference to the *difference* between the actual interest paid (if any) and interest at a rate equal to the "official rate". This rate has not yet been defined, but it is to be prescribed from time to time by the Treasury by statutory instrument. In this connection the following exchange was reported in *Hansard* of 27th May 1977.

"Mr. George Cunningham asked the Chancellor of the Exchequer when the official rate of interest for 1978-79 will be prescribed for the purpose of Section 66 of the Finance Act 1976; and if he will make a statement.

Mr. Robert Sheldon: An order prescribing the rate will be introduced in the House in about October this year. The rate will be determined in relation to the rate of interest which a credit-worthy personal borrower might have to pay on a bank overdraft. The rate in the order will take effect from the start of the fiscal year 1978-79 and will remain in force until further notice. The intention will be that that rate should remain in force at least until the end of 1978-79, but, if market rates should change substantially between the introduction of the order and the middle of 1978-79, a further order may be introduced to change the official rate either immediately or from the start of the fiscal year 1979-80."

Effective Date

As stated above, the provisions taxing "interest free" loans as a benefit in kind do not take effect until 6th April 1978. Furthermore, for the tax years 1978/79 and 1979/80 the amount taxable will only be equal to *one-half* of the prospective benefit.

Example

Peter Piper, editor of Eating and Drinking News Ltd, receives a loan from his employer of £10,000, on which he pays 1% interest (£100 a year). If the "official rate" is eventually prescribed as 10%, it will be considered that Peter ought to pay £1,000 a year interest. Because he has only paid £100, he will be taxable each year on £900 as a benefit in kind under Schedule E. He cannot be chargeable for the fiscal year 1977/78, and for the following two fiscal years, 1978/79 and 1979/80, he will only be chargeable on £450 (i.e. half-rate). The full effect of this provision will not therefore be felt until 6th April 1980.

Relief

Relief is available in certain defined situations, the most important being:

i)   If the value of the benefit does not exceed £50 a year. If for example the official rate is prescribed at 10%, this will mean that as of 1980/81 loans of £500 may be made without tax charge.

ii) If the interest on the loan *would have* qualified for tax relief had it been paid. For example, if an executive is granted a loan to buy his principal private residence, in circumstances where the loan would qualify for mortgage relief, the benefit of the interest free loan will not be taxable.

Ascertainment of Liability

The position regarding interest must be ascertained over a complete fiscal year. Tax will be chargeable according to the rate of interest paid (if any), the period of time any loan is outstanding during the year, and so on.

2.   Loans Written Off

The legislation also imposes a tax charge where a loan is written off.

Example

Clive Roberts works for New Antiques for Old Limited, who make him a loan of £10,000. The obligation to repay the loan is waived by his employers. In that year, Clive will be taxable on the amount of the loan written off, since it will be regarded as an emolument under Schedule E.

Additional Points

i)   The provision relating to loans written off is effective from 6th April 1976.

ii)   These provisions apply whether or not the loan carries interest at a nil or low rate, and also if the loan interest would have qualified for income tax relief had any interest been paid. Even though an executive may have left the employment of the company granting him a loan, the provisions still apply. He will be "deemed" to have remained an employee — the only exception being his death.

iii)   As usual, the rules apply if the loan is made to a member of the executive's family etc. and then is written off.

PART III — MISCELLANEOUS ITEMS

Apart from "golden handshakes" and beneficial loan arrangements, there are other types of capital incentive which may be given to executives, or indeed to employees generally.

i) It may be possible to give a new employee an "incentive" to join one's company. In the case of Pritchard v. Arundale, a chartered accountant became friendly with the managing director of one of his client companies and was eventually offered the position of joint managing director with the group. As an incentive or "inducement" to him to give up his private practice and to work for the group, he was offered valuable shares in the company free. These he accepted and subsequently he took up the position.

It was held by the Courts that the payment was not a form of disguised remuneration but was a *genuine* incentive or inducement to attract the accountant. It was held not to be taxable.

Although this principle may no longer be effective in relation to company shares, it would still seem to be valid for other capital payments.

ii) A voluntary payment made on the surrender of a right, say holiday entitlement, is not taxable.

However, if the surrender of the right concerns remuneration (i.e. payment accepted in return for working for a smaller salary) then such payment would be taxable, as established in the case of Tilley v. Wales.

iii) The Inland Revenue is normally generous towards employees who are moving jobs, and consequently locations, within a group of companies. Lump sum payments designed to defray the cost of upheaval — new furnishings, removal expenses and settling-in allowances — will not be taxable provided they are kept within reasonable bounds.

This principle is particularly beneficial when a company is trying to attract new staff from overseas, since it can provide generous settling-in allowances etc. which are free of income tax.

iv) A company may sometimes be able to put its executives in a favourable position to build up capital outside the company.

This sometimes occurs in relation to Lloyds membership: a company may be able to arrange for its senior executives to become members at Lloyds by guaranteeing the capital worth of the executives in question.

CHAPTER 9

WORKING AND TRAVELLING OVERSEAS

The tax position of UK residents working and travelling overseas will here be analysed under the following main headings:

PART I – BACKGROUND INFORMATION

PART II – THE 1977 FINANCE ACT CHANGES IN DETAIL

PART III – MISCELLANEOUS ITEMS

Overseas considerations also impinge on other chapters of this book; for example, Chapter 7 (Executive Share Option and Incentive Schemes), Chapter 8 (Golden Handshakes and other Tax Effective Capital Payments) and Chapter 10 (Pension and Life Assurance Arrangements). Since these subjects have each been given a chapter of their own, the overseas considerations affecting them have been dealt with in the appropriate chapter and *not* here. The subject is so complicated that confusion may arise if too many different aspects of working overseas are analysed in one chapter.

Furthermore, it should be emphasised that this chapter deals solely with taxation, and is not concerned with the UK Exchange Control implications of working outside the Scheduled Territories. Naturally, all UK residents taking up employment overseas should acquaint themselves with the Bank of England's regulations to ensure that they are not in breach of them.

The rules applicable to overseas emoluments do not depend on the status or emolument level of the person concerned, and consequently throughout this chapter the term "employee" will be used to describe anyone potentially taxable under Schedule E. Thus a director will be classified as an employee for the purposes of this chapter and the word "employment" will include the word "office" where appropriate.

PART I — BACKGROUND INFORMATION

Overseas Residence

As explained in Chapter 2, Schedule E income tax can be levied under any one of three cases, depending on the residential status of the recipient and the source of the emoluments in question.

Consequently, when a person goes overseas to work for a complete tax year, in circumstances where he is no longer regarded as "resident" in the UK, he should not be liable to tax in the UK on emoluments paid from overseas, since residence is a vital factor in making emoluments liable to tax in the UK. The only liability to UK tax would be in respect of emoluments derived from the UK, when the taxpayer in question may come within the scope of Schedule E Case II (as explained in Chapter 2).

Where a taxpayer leaves the UK to work overseas on a full-time service contract, and will be working overseas for at least a complete tax year, the present Inland Revenue practice is to regard that person as not resident and not ordinarily resident in the UK from the day following the date of departure until the day preceding the day of return. This practice is beneficial in that:—

a)   The fiscal year is split into two, and full personal allowances can be set off against that part of the taxable income falling in the part-year of "residence",

and   b)   The immediate acquisition of "non-ordinarily resident" status can be helpful in the context of capital gains tax liability, in that disposals can be made following departure to take up employment abroad, with complete exemption from liability to UK capital gains tax.

From the above, it will be seen that if a person can become non-resident, he will not be taxable on overseas emoluments. However, the majority of people who work overseas may not spend a complete fiscal year outside the UK and thus remain potentially exposed to full Schedule E liability on overseas emoluments. This chapter is mainly concerned with people who fall within this category.

Old Regulations

Until 1974 it was a relatively simple exercise for UK resident taxpayers to avoid income tax under Schedule E on overseas emoluments. This was because the laws were then framed in such a way that only *remittances* of offshore emoluments were taxable. If there was no remittance (actual or constructive) there could be no tax on the overseas emoluments, even though the recipient taxpayer remained fully resident (and ordinarily resident) in the UK throughout the period under consideration.

To take a simple example, the generally-adopted scheme was that a UK resident taxpayer with a substantial source of overseas Schedule E taxable income would bring the emoluments back to say Jersey or Guernsey and place them on deposit with a Channel Islands bank, since overseas earnings must be remitted back into sterling "without delay" under the Bank of England regulations.

Provided the funds in the Channel Islands were not directly or indirectly transmitted to the UK, they would be free of tax.

It is a fundamental principle of UK taxation law that, for income to be taxable, there must be some "source" of income during the fiscal year. Thus it would be arranged that the employee terminated his employment contract on say 31st March in one fiscal year, and would then remit the overseas emoluments from the Channel Islands on say 10th June in a subsequent fiscal year. Because *at the date of remittance* the Schedule E taxpayer had no "employment", there could by definition be no source of income in the year of remittance, and thus the original income would be entirely exempt from UK tax liability.

Allegedly because of the revelations arising from the Lonrho affair, where quite substantial overseas emoluments were derived on a tax advantageous basis, the law applicable to overseas emoluments taxable under Schedule E was amended in the 1974 Finance Act.

1974 Finance Act

The change in the law substituted an "arising" basis of taxation in respect of overseas emoluments for the old "remittances" basis. As explained in Chapter 2, this meant that, with the one exception of Schedule E Case III source income, income from overseas employment was now taxable as and when it arose overseas, and the date of remittance to the UK became quite irrelevant. Thus, under the new regulations there was no point in bringing funds back to Jersey or Guernsey and leaving them there until the employment ceased, since the taxpayer was taxable on an identical basis whether the funds were brought back to the UK immediately or subsequently.

Although the 1974 Finance Act provided that income was to be taxable on an arising basis, reliefs were introduced to give tax benefits in respect of time spent overseas. Where the employee could show that he was overseas for a complete year, which did not need to coincide with the fiscal year, 100% of the emoluments were free of tax. If the employee was not overseas for a complete year but was overseas for part of the time, then 25% of those emoluments were free of tax and the balance taxable in the ordinary way.

As time went on, it became apparent that the rules introduced by the Finance Act 1974 were defective in certain respects, and this led to the amendments introduced by the 1977 Finance Act. The major defects in the 1974 Finance Act were as follows:—

i) Firstly, the relief was only available where it could be shown that the *whole of the duties* of the particular office or employment were performed overseas. If the UK Inland Revenue could prove that any *part* of the duties was performed *in the UK* then the whole relief was forfeit.

The only exception was if it could be shown that the duties performed in the UK were merely "incidental" to the overseas duties. This frequently meant that disputes arose between the taxpayer and the Inland Revenue as to whether a particular duty could properly be described as incidental. The problem of whether a duty is "incidental" is still with us under the 1977 Finance Act, and a brief commentary on incidental duties is contained in Part III of this chapter.

ii)   As a corollary to the above point, it followed that where a
       Schedule E taxpayer had a UK job of which a substantial part of
       the duties involved going overseas, that UK taxpayer would
       receive no relief in respect of time spent overseas since that time
       was regarded as part and parcel of his UK job. In these circum-
       stances, it was necessary to attempt to split the employment into
       two parts, one of which was clearly referable solely to the UK
       duties, and the other solely to the overseas duties, none of which
       were performed in the UK.

iii)   Problems frequently arose over subsistence payments. As a simple
       example, if taxpayer F was employed by Tax Avoiders Limited in
       London and by Tax Avoiders (Paris) Limited in France, the Inland
       Revenue sought to tax subsistence payments made in France (e.g.
       overnight hotel accommodation etc.), arguing that payments of
       this nature were benefits in kind from the overseas job. It is
       however understood that the Inland Revenue has recently decided
       to amend its extra statutory concessions — A5 and A25 — to
       counteract the problem described. This revised practice will there-
       fore be effective for the years covered by the 1974 Finance Act,
       that is to say, fiscal years 1974/75 to 1976/77 inclusive.

iv)   Lastly, where an employee was working overseas for a period of
       time he may well have wished to visit his family in the UK, or
       alternatively have his family visit him abroad. In either case, pay-
       ment by the employer of travelling expenses was usually classified
       as a "personal" as opposed to a "business" expense and was thus
       potentially taxable as a benefit in kind.

For these and other reasons the 1974 legislation has been set aside
and a completely new set of rules has been introduced by the 1977
Finance Act. The new provisions are considered in Part II of this
chapter.

PART II — THE 1977 FINANCE ACT CHANGES IN DETAIL

For convenience the new rules will be summarised under several main headings. At the outset, however, it must be made clear that these new regulations only apply to employees taxable under Schedule E Case I, that is to say, people who are both "resident and ordinarily resident" in the UK. They do not apply to Cases II and III of Schedule E. As explained previously, where a person leaves the UK in circumstances such that he is not resident (or indeed ordinarily resident) during the particular tax year, then his overseas emoluments will not be taxable under the provisions of Schedule E and these emoluments will therefore be free of UK tax *without recourse* to the 1977 Finance Act regulations described here.

Readers who wish to inspect the text of the new legislation for overseas emoluments are referred to Section 31 and Schedule 7 of the Act. The rules relating to travelling expenses only are contained in Section 32 of the Act.

1. 100% Deduction

Where the duties of an employment are performed wholly *or partly* outside the UK, and those duties are performed during a *qualifying period* of at least 365 days, then the whole of the emoluments properly attributable to those overseas duties are exempt from taxation.

Note in particular that:—

a) The relief is given even though part of the duties are performed in the UK and only part overseas.

b) The qualifying period of at least 365 days need not coincide with a fiscal year. For example, a taxpayer going overseas on 1st June 1977 and returning to the UK on 15th June 1978 would be regarded as having spent a qualifying period of at least 365 days overseas for this purpose, even though he or she was not out of the UK for a complete fiscal year.

c) The term "qualifying period" means *either* complete days of absence from the UK *or* "deemed" days of absence.

As regards the latter, certain days spent in the UK can be treated as days spent overseas provided they meet two conditions.

Firstly, any one period spent in the UK must not exceed 62 consecutive days, and secondly, the days spent in the UK must not exceed 1/6th of the total period under consideration. If *either* of these two conditions is not met, then the days spent in the UK will serve to break up the total period, which may not then reach the important minimum of 365 days.

Example

1. John Taxpayer goes overseas to work for 9 months, comes back to the UK for 3 months, and then goes overseas to work for a further 9 months before returning to the UK permanently.

    If one adds up the 9 months spent overseas, plus the 3 months in the UK followed by another 9 months overseas, the total period under consideration is 21 months. Of this period, only 3 months, or 1/7th, has been spent in the UK, and thus these 3 months are initially regarded as "deemed" days of absence, as described. *However*, 3 months in the UK not broken up by any overseas periods totals 93 consecutive days, and therefore John Taxpayer fails the "62-day" test. Consequently, each period of 9 months must be considered in isolation, and the 3 intervening months will not be deemed "overseas days". Thus on this basis the 100% deduction will not be available, although the 25% deduction described below would be given.

2. Freda Taxing goes overseas to work for 3 months, comes back to the UK for a month, goes overseas for 4 months, comes back to the UK·for 2 months and then goes overseas for a further 2 months before returning to the UK permanently. She has thus in theory been "outside" the UK for the 365-day minimum period. The time Freda spent back in the UK does not fall foul of the 62 consecutive day test (i.e. 2 months). However, during the year the total period of her presence in the UK has amounted to 3 months, out of a potential "qualifying period" of 12 months. This means that one quarter (3/12) of the total period has been spent

in the UK, which of course exceeds the maximum permissible proportion of 1/6th. Freda Taxing will not be entitled to the 100% deduction because she has breached the "1/6th" test, but the 25% deduction described below should be available in respect of each tour of overseas duty.

It is important to understand that the Inland Revenue, in order to establish whether the 62-day test or the 1/6th test are being breached, will look at a taxpayer's movements on a cumulative basis. Therefore, two taxpayers could spend the same amount of time in the UK and overseas, but the *order* in which the overseas duties occur would determine whether the 100% deduction is available. The following will illustrate this point:—

Illustration

Taxpayer A spends 5 months outside the UK, 2 months in the UK and the remaining 5 months overseas. The total period under consideration is thus 12 months, of which 2 months have been spent in the UK. The 62 consecutive day test and the 1/6th total period test are therefore satisfied, and the period of 2 months in the UK is "deemed" to be a period of absence.

Taxpayer B spends the same total period overseas and in the UK, but it is made up differently. He spends 1 month overseas, followed by 1 month back in the UK, followed by 2 months overseas, followed by 1 month back in the UK, followed by the remaining 7 months overseas, before returning to the UK permanently.

In determining whether the 1/6th test and the 62 consecutive day tests have been breached, the Inland Revenue will consider each UK period which is straddled by an overseas period. Thus they will look at the 1 month spent overseas, the 1 month in the UK, followed by the 2 months spent overseas. This is a total period of 4 months, of which 1 month has been spent in the UK. The 62-day test is therefore satisfied but the 1/6th test is not, and this means that the whole period of 4 months under consideration cannot be deemed to have been totally overseas, since one-quarter of the total has been spent in the UK. In consequence, the first month of absence is ignored, and the succeeding calculation will therefore commence with the 2 months of absence overseas, the 1 month spent in the UK and the 7 months of absence overseas. During this period the 1/6th test is met and so is the 62 consecutive day test. However, the period totals only 10 months in all, less than the minimum figure of 365 days, and the 100% deduction cannot therefore be given.

From the above it will be seen that it is important to plan carefully one's days of absence from and presence in the UK respectively, since two people spending the same total time overseas may nevertheless have quite different *taxable* incomes.

Before leaving the subject of the favourable 100% deduction, the following additional points should be mentioned:—

i)   Any payment made on terminal leave will be identified with the overseas period of absence and will thus be potentially tax exempt. For example, if a taxpayer has worked overseas for 18 months and on termination of that employment is immediately paid say 3 months' money for "leave", that leave payment will be classified as part of the emoluments qualifying for the 100% deduction. This is so even though the taxpayer may return to the UK and spend his leave there.

ii) Although the changes made by the Finance Act 1977 to the law in this area were not effective until the fiscal year 1977/78, it specifically provides that, for the purposes of the 100% deduction, a period of absence overseas commencing prior to 6th April 1977 may nevertheless count in calculating the 365-day minimum. Thus if a taxpayer went overseas on 1st January 1977 and returns to the UK on 2nd January 1978, the earnings attributable to this period will be tax exempt — provided of course that the 1/6th and 62 consecutive day tests are satisfied — even though the change in the tax law was only effective from 6th April 1977.

iii) Specific anti-avoidance rules (see over) have been enacted, to ensure that only a just proportion of one's total emoluments qualifies for the 100% deduction.

iv)   To qualify for a day of absence, the taxpayer must be outside the UK at midnight on the day in question.

2.   25% Deduction — Part Performance

Where the 100% deduction described above is not available, the emoluments under consideration may nevertheless qualify for the 25% deduction. For example, if a taxpayer derives £1,000 from an overseas employment contract and the conditions specified below are met, he will be taxable on £750 at his ordinary tax rates, but the balance of £250 will be tax free. Where a person has a job which he performs wholly *or partly* overseas, this relief will only be available provided he accumulates at least 30 qualifying *days* during the fiscal year. If he only accumulates 29 days during the year then he will receive no allowance, but if he clocks up 1 more day, then 25% of the emoluments properly attributable to those overseas duties will be tax exempt, as described. Readers may feel that there should be some graduated scale between the 30-day absence and 25% deduction and the 365 days of absence and the 100% deduction. But although attempts were made during the debates on the 1977 Finance Act to obtain progressive relief (e.g. 50% after 6 months, 75% after 9 months, etc.), the government would not agree.

Clearly, the definition of the term "qualifying day" is important, and this was modified during the Finance Act debates in Parliament. The greatest problem facing the drafters of the Act was to restrict the relief to the situation where someone is actually working overseas, yet still to make "reasonable" allowances for the fact that people overseas would not normally work on the weekends, nor indeed on public holidays. A qualifying day is therefore a day of *absence* from the UK (i.e. at midnight) which fulfils one or more of the following conditions:

i)   A day *substantially devoted to* the performance outside the UK of the duties of the employment (or indeed the duties of that and other employments),

or ii)   a day which is one of at least 7 *consecutive days* on which the person concerned is absent from the UK for the purposes of performing such duties and which (taken as a whole) are *substantially devoted* to the performance of such duties,

or iii)   a day spent travelling in (or for the purposes of) the performance of the duties outside the UK.

Unfortunately the phrase "substantially devoted" is not defined, and therefore a commonsense approach must be taken. From definition (ii) above, it is for example quite clear that where a person spends 7 *consecutive days* overseas and works on all the normal working days, but not at the weekends, the whole 7-day period will be classified as qualifying days. However, if a person went overseas to work for say 10 days and then took 10 days holiday overseas immediately afterwards, the 10 days of holiday would obviously not be "substantially devoted" to the *performance* of the duties and would thus not qualify for relief.

It must be emphasised that:

a)   The 30 qualifying days are aggregate days and not consecutive days. They are considered on a fiscal year by fiscal year basis.

b)   Specific anti-avoidance rules have been introduced (see below) to prevent more than a reasonable proportion of total emoluments being attributed to the overseas duties entitled to the 25% deduction.

c)   Time spent travelling can count as a qualifying day.

3.   25% Deduction — Separate Employments

It is popularly thought that the 25% allowance is only available when at least 30 days are spent overseas. THIS IS NOT TRUE.

Provided two conditions are fulfilled, the 25% deduction can be given *regardless* of the time spent outside the UK (i.e. even 1 day overseas can qualify for the deduction).

The two conditions are as follows:—

a)   Firstly, the duties of that employment must be performed *wholly outside* the UK. This should be contrasted with the reliefs mentioned in 1 and 2 above, where relief is now given when only part of the duties are performed abroad.

Thus, if the Inland Revenue can show that any part of the duties are performed in the UK, other than incidental duties, the relief under this heading will be lost and the taxpayer must fall back on the 30 qualifying day limitation.

b)   The employment must be with an employer who is resident outside the UK. Thus the employment cannot be with a UK taxpaying company, but must be with a foreign company; although a company established in say Jersey or Guernsey would suffice.

It is interesting that the 25% deduction is available under this heading without the necessity of having any "qualifying" days as such. Thus, provided all the duties of the employment are performed outside the UK, the relief would seem to be available even though the taxpayer may not have been absent from the UK at midnight on the day concerned, as is necessary for the two exemptions previously described.

4.   Anti-Avoidance

As readers may appreciate, it is almost impossible nowadays for any new fiscal legislation to be introduced without it including numerous anti-avoidance provisions. The Finance Act 1977 is no exception, and there follows an analysis of the anti-avoidance rules applicable to the 100% and 25% deductions mentioned above.

The wording is complicated, but basically the Act provides that the anti-avoidance rules apply when either the employment under consideration, or an employment which can be "associated" therewith, is not performed *wholly* outside the UK. For this purpose an employment can be said to be "associated" if it is either with the same person or with an associated person, that is to say, companies under common control, partnerships under common control, and so on.

Consequently, we will not be concerned with the anti-avoidance rules if the duties of the employment under consideration and the duties of any associated employment are performed wholly outside the UK. The following examples may be helpful:

Example

a)   John Taxpayer works for Tax Avoiders Limited in London, and also has a position on the board of their wholly-owned French subsidiary Tax Avoiders (de Paris) Limited. The two jobs are quite independent, and the duties of John Taxpayer's UK job are performed wholly in the UK and the duties of his Paris job wholly in France. Nevertheless the companies are "associated", in that they are under common control. This means that the UK Inland Revenue may invoke the anti-avoidance provisions to ensure that only a reasonable proportion (in their eyes) of John Taxpayer's total emoluments is attributable to the overseas position, and thus will probably qualify for the 25% deduction.

b)   Let us now assume that John Taxpayer only has one employment, the duties of which he performs partly in the UK and partly overseas. Although in this case there is no associated employment, it is clear that the duties of the "relevant employment" are performed partly in the UK, and therefore the Inland Revenue will invoke the anti-avoidance rules.

c)   Assume that John Taxpayer works for Tax Avoiders Limited in London and also for Newman Incorporated in the Bahamas. The companies (Newman Incorporated and Tax Avoiders Limited) have no connection whatsoever and thus the "associated" provisions cannot be invoked. Furthermore, the employment which may qualify for the deduction is that with Newman Incorporated, which for the purposes of the anti-avoidance rules is of course the "relevant" employment. Since the duties of this employment are performed *wholly outside* the UK, the Inland Revenue is not entitled to invoke the anti-avoidance rules, since they cannot bring this employment or any associated employment within the scope of the regulations.

The anti-avoidance rules are as follows:—

100% Deduction

This deduction will only be available in respect of that proportion of the total emoluments for that year which can be shown to be *reasonable*, having regard to "the nature of and time devoted to the duties performed outside and in the UK respectively and to all other relevant circumstances".

25% Deduction

If the employee is only entitled to the 25% deduction — either by accumulating 30 qualifying days *or* by having a separate employment with an overseas employer, the duties of which are performed wholly overseas — the anti-avoidance rules are somewhat different.

Initially the legislation states that only the "prescribed proportion" of the emoluments qualify, *unless* the taxpayer can show that a larger proportion than this strict *pro rata* calculation can be justified, "having regard to the nature of and time devoted to the duties performed outside and in the UK respectively and to all other relevant circumstances". The prescribed proportion is a fraction, the numerator of which is overseas days and the denominator of which is usually 365.

The Inland Revenue will begin by comparing the number of "qualifying days" spent outside the UK with the total number of days under consideration; normally 365, but obviously less if the relevant employment, or associated employment, is held for less than a year. The anti-avoidance rules are somewhat curiously drafted, in the sense that they relate "qualifying days" to the 365-day period; it will be remembered that the 25% deduction given to duties performed wholly overseas with a non-resident employer was not dependent on "qualifying days". However, the anti-avoidance provisions are drafted by reference to qualifying days of absence.

Examples

The anti-avoidance rules can best be illustrated by a few typical examples. These are concerned with the 25% deduction, since this also brings out the anti-avoidance wording applicable to the 100% deduction (i.e. "such amount as is shown to be reasonable having regard to, etc.").

1. A UK sales manager is appointed, and during the fiscal year he spends 10 months in the UK and 2 months "qualifying days" overseas. He is paid £12,000 per annum.

    The UK Inland Revenue will begin by contending that since he only works for 1/6th of his total time overseas and is paid £12,000 a year, the portion of his income attributable to the overseas duties is £2,000. Since he would only be entitled to the 25% deduction, this means that £500 (i.e. one-quarter of £2,000) will be exempt from UK tax, and that the balance of his income, totalling £11,500, will be taxable in the ordinary way.

2. Assume that the sales manager spends his 2 months overseas working in Hong Kong, and that in addition to his ordinary salary he receives commission payments during the year of £24,000. Owing to a magnificent piece of exporting, no less than three-quarters (£18,000) of the total commission of £24,000 relates to the genuine sales of goods in Hong Kong. Here, therefore, it can clearly be shown that the entire £18,000 should be referable to the overseas duties, rather than merely one-sixth of £24,000 (£4,000), a figure based on the percentage of total time spent overseas. Thus, although the Inland Revenue may begin their calculations on a simple time-apportionment basis, in this case it can genuinely be proved that £18,000 of the total bonus payments relate to offshore work, and therefore the Revenue would be prepared to accept that the £18,000 qualified for the 25% deduction.

3. Let us now assume that our sales manager earning £12,000 a year works in France for 2 months, as sales director of his company's French subsidiary. Owing to the sales manager's expertise, contacts, etc., and indeed because of the generally higher level of salaries in France, it would cost the French subsidiary £5,500 to hire someone of his calibre locally.

In these circumstances the Inland Revenue is prepared to accept that £5,500 should properly be considered as the sales manager's overseas emoluments, rather than the strict *pro rata* figure of £2,000.

5.   Evidence

One question which is frequently asked in relation to overseas duties is "How does the Inland Revenue know how much time I have spent working overseas?"

The answer is simply that whenever a taxpayer is claiming a deduction or allowance for tax purposes, it is up to the *taxpayer* to satisfy the Inland Revenue that in the particular circumstances of the case the deduction or allowance is valid. Thus the Revenue must be happy with the evidence given to them that in the circumstances relief under Finance Act 1977 is available. Clearly, practice will vary between local Inspectors of Taxes, but executives would be well advised to keep full details of their overseas travelling. Such details should perhaps be recorded in a business diary, which would specify the periods spent overseas, the duties then performed, and so on. This diary could be supported by airline or shipping tickets. Having made a claim for relief, the taxpayer may be asked to submit *any evidence* which he holds in support of his claim, and in many cases the Inspector of Taxes might receive from the employer evidence in support of claims made by the employees.

A sensible course of action would therefore be for employers to approach their local Inspectors of Taxes to ascertain in advance the detailed evidence required by that particular Inspector. The employer may then advise his employees accordingly.

6.   Aircraft and Ships

One further amendment introduced by the Finance Act is small in itself but very important for the people concerned. It is now possible for employees working for international airlines, shipping companies and the like to obtain some measure of relief for the time they spend outside the UK. Hitherto (under Section 184 T.A.1970), any UK resident performing duties on a ship or aircraft which either started or ended its voyage in the UK was regarded as having performed all those duties in the UK, and thus no relief was available.

Now, journeys outside the UK will qualify, and such employees may expect to obtain the 25% deduction, provided they accumulate at least 30 qualifying days overseas — since part of their duties would be performed in the UK and part overseas.

7. PAYE

It is obviously helpful from a cash-flow point of view if the taxpayer can arrange for provisional relief in respect of qualifying overseas income to be written into his coding notice from the outset, rather than be obliged to wait until the end of the fiscal year and then claim back overpaid tax from the Inland Revenue.

It is understood that relief will be available through the PAYE system, and any employers wishing to consider this method of relief should therefore contact the local Inspector of Taxes for details. Clearly, certain information and undertakings will be required by the Inspector before he grants provisional PAYE relief, and there should also be a comprehensive analysis at the end of the fiscal year to confirm that the PAYE estimates are correct in practice.

8. Travelling

The new travelling regulations may be summarised as follows:—

a) Where the taxpayer is both resident and ordinarily resident in the UK (i.e. Schedule E Case I), any travelling expenses incurred in leaving tne UK to take up an overseas employment, or travelling back to the UK on the termination of that employment, are regarded as totally tax deductible for Schedule E purposes. If the expense is borne by the employer, then it would not of course be a taxable benefit in kind.

b) If the Schedule E Case I taxpayer goes overseas for one employment and then proceeds from there to another employment overseas, the cost of travelling between the two places is regarded as a tax deductible expense. Similarly, if this payment is made by the employer, it will not rank as a taxable benefit in kind.

c)   Where a Schedule E Case I taxpayer is working overseas and his employer meets the cost of board and lodging, or alternatively reimburses the employee with the cost of board and lodging paid for by the employee, the amount of such cost or reimbursement will not be taxable on the employee concerned.

It is curious that no relief is given if the employee incurs the cost of board and lodgings but the employer does not reimburse it. This point was raised during the Commons debates, and the explanation given was that this was intended to stop employees incurring totally unreasonable board and lodging expenses. The implication is that if the employer is prepared to reimburse the expenses, then by definition the expenses would not be "unreasonable"!

d)   It should be noted that the expenses classified under (a), (b) and (c) above are only non-taxable to the extent that the expense can be shown to be properly related to a business function. If the Inland Revenue can show that all or part of the expense has a "non-business" flavour, then all or a proportion of the expense incurred will be taxable.

e)   Where a Schedule E Case I taxpayer is working overseas for a *continuous period* of at least 60 days, the employer may pay, or reimburse to the employee, certain family travelling costs without such payment or reimbursement being regarded as a taxable benefit to the employee concerned.

Once again, there is the rather curious provision that the benefit is only available if it is borne by the employer or reimbursed by the employer to the employee. If the employee incurs the expense himself, with no reimbursement by the employer, then the payment by the employee will not be deductible for tax purposes.

The exemption extends to travel "facilities" made available to a resident spouse and/or children who either accompany the employee out at the inception of the trip (or back on termination) or alternatively travel out to visit the employee during his period overseas. However, the employer may not finance more than two return journeys by the same person during any one year of assessment. For this purpose the term "child" includes a stepchild, an adopted child and an illegitimate child, but in all cases the child must be under the age of 18 at the commencement of the *outward journey*.

During the parliamentary debates on this aspect of the Finance Act 1977 it was pointed out that it might be cheaper for all concerned if the employee could return to the UK to visit his spouse and children, and this provision is now contained in the Finance Act.

The term travel "facilities" is not defined, but it is felt that it can reasonably include hotel accommodation *en route* and not merely the air fare.

PART III – MISCELLANEOUS ITEMS

1.   Overseas Tax and Unilateral Relief

Anyone taking up employment overseas may well be exposing themselves to an overseas tax charge, and may indeed come within the scope of the overseas territory's social security system as well. Anyone taking up employment, even for a brief period, should acquaint themselves with any potential taxation and social security liability in the overseas territory. Often the provisions of a Double Taxation Treaty will apply; see the next note.

Where a person pays tax to an overseas jurisdiction, the UK Inland Revenue will grant what is termed unilateral relief, in the absence of relief given by a Double Taxation Treaty. This is so irrespective of the fact that part of the emoluments may be exempt from UK taxation under the rules described above.

Example

John Smith works part of the time for Tax Avoiders Limited in the Principality of Eldorado. During the fiscal year he received £2,000 from the subsidiary in Eldorado.

Eldorado levies a flat rate tax of 30% on income, which means that John Smith will pay £600 to the taxation authorities there.

As far as the UK Inland Revenue is concerned, John Smith will be entitled to the 25% deduction already explained. This means that of the £2,000 salary, £500 will be free of tax and the balance of £1,500 taxable. If John Smith's marginal rate of income tax is 50%, the UK tax applicable to his offshore emoluments will therefore be £750 (i.e. 50% of £1,500). However, since he has paid £600 in tax to the Eldorado authorities, his additional UK tax burden will only be £150 (i.e. the difference). This is so even though £500 of the income from Eldorado is specifically exempt from UK taxation by virtue of the 1977 Finance Act.

2.   Double Taxation Treaties

The UK depends upon international trade and in consequence the UK Inland Revenue authorities have negotiated numerous Double Taxation Treaties with overseas territories. The object of a Double Taxation Treaty is to make matters simpler for all concerned and also to spell out, in any given circumstances, which territory is entitled to tax on certain items of income, capital and so on.

Double Taxation Treaties are important, since by virtue of Section 497 T.A.1970 the terms of any Treaty override UK domestic law. Thus if the two are at variance, the terms of the Treaty will apply. This being the case, anyone taking up overseas employment should ascertain whether the UK has a Treaty in force with that overseas territory. If so, the Treaty should be carefully analysed to establish whether it applies to the particular circumstances of the individual.

Although such Treaties nowadays tend to follow a certain pattern, the "O.E.C.D. model treaty", one must not automatically assume that the terms of a particular Treaty follow exactly the terms of the model agreement. However, most Treaties enable directors' fees to be taxable in both countries, whereas income from *employment* is generally only taxable in one of the contracting states.

3.   Benefits In Kind

This chapter has discussed the attitude of the UK Revenue to the taxation of overseas emoluments, and the term "emoluments" obviously includes benefits in kind.

In consequence, if a person is working overseas in circumstances such that he qualifies for the 100% deduction, it would clearly be advantageous to maximise the benefit in kind payments, since these will also qualify for the total tax exemption. In fact, the employer could provide almost any conceivable benefit in kind without thought of taxation repercussions, since all *emoluments* would be tax free.

Likewise, if the employee works overseas in circumstances such that the 25% deduction can be given, then this deduction would also extend to the taxation of benefits in kind.

4.   Incidental Duties

As explained earlier in this chapter, the term "incidental duties" is important. For example, a claim for the 25% deduction, for work performed wholly overseas for a non-resident employer, would not be granted if part of those duties had been performed in the UK.

Whether or not a duty can be said to be "incidental" depends on the facts of the case, and it is difficult to lay down firm rules. However, while it is primarily the nature of the duties rather than the time spent on them which determines whether they are regarded as "incidental", the Inland Revenue would usually consider any duties which took up more than 3 months of a fiscal year as *not* being incidental to the overseas duties.

Subject to this 3-month rule, the Inland Revenue would regard the following as "incidental" duties:

a)   Visits to the UK solely for training purposes.

b)   Visits to the UK merely to report to UK employers or to receive fresh instructions.

Conversely, a company director who usually worked overseas could not claim the attendance of a UK board meeting as being incidental to the overseas duties.

5.   Foreign Emoluments

In Chapter 2 it was mentioned that some relief could be given in the taxation of emoluments under Schedule E Cases I or II in respect of what were termed "foreign emoluments".

Briefly, foreign emoluments are the emoluments of a person not domiciled in the UK which are derived from an office or employment with an employer who is resident outside the UK.

Where a person can show that he does receive foreign emoluments as defined, then normally one half of such emoluments is exempt from UK taxation and the other half is taxable in the ordinary way. The only exception to this rule occurs where the employee has resided in the UK (for tax purposes) for at least 9 out of the preceding 10 years, when only 25% of the foreign emoluments are tax free and the remaining 75% are taxable.

Presumably, few readers of this book will qualify under the foreign emolument heading since, although they may work for an overseas employer, they will normally be domiciled in the UK for tax purposes.

6.   Non-Taxation Factors

Although the main advantages of an overseas employment from a UK point of view are the tax savings, there are some non-taxation benefits to be derived. The following are worthy of note:

a)   A person with an overseas employment contract is usually given the facility of having his income or salary expressed in a non-sterling currency. Although under Bank of England regulations such income must normally be remitted to the Scheduled Territories, the taxpayer is guaranteed against a fall in his international living standards. A good illustration would be the position of an employee who negotiated an employment contract expressed in Deutschmarks a couple of years ago.

b)   An overseas employment contract can be particularly advantageous if pay restrictions are introduced in the UK. By definition,

UK pay restrictions apply to UK companies, but if a taxpayer has an employment contract with an overseas company, he cannot be prevented from receiving salary increments from this non-UK source.

c)   Depending on the precise nature of the employment contract, and particularly on other UK employments which the taxpayer may have, income from a foreign source may be paid gross, without deduction of PAYE tax at source. This could be an advantage to the employee's cash flow.

CHAPTER 10

PENSION AND LIFE ASSURANCE ARRANGEMENTS

This is such a vast topic that only the major aspects can be dealt with in the space of one chapter. Quite apart from considerations such as cost and impact on staff morale, a group pension and life assurance scheme must be examined from two quite separate *technical* points of view:

i) Firstly, according to the rules and regulations laid down by the Inland Revenue, will it be "exempt approved" for taxation purposes?

ii) Secondly, are the benefits provided sufficient to enable it to be used for "contracting out" of the State scheme (the so-called "Castle Scheme")

These two considerations restrict the freedom of a company to offer a package of death and retirement benefits suited to the particular needs of its employees. To contract out of the "Castle Scheme", thereby reducing the national insurance contributions of both employees and employers, the scheme must guarantee a certain *minimum* level of benefits.

However, to satisfy the Inland Revenue for tax exemption purposes (which is probably more important), the benefits cannot exceed certain maxima. Thus there is both a floor and a ceiling on the benefits which can be provided.

Although the Inland Revenue attitude towards pension schemes in the UK and the requirements for contracting out are the two most important subjects to be dealt with in this chapter, reference will also be made to self-employed pensions and also to certain overseas aspects. This chapter will examine the following main areas:

> PART I   – INLAND REVENUE CONSIDERATIONS
>
> PART II – STATE SCHEME CONSIDERATIONS
>
> PART III – SELF EMPLOYED
>
> PART IV – OVERSEAS ASPECTS

No distinction is made between employees, directors etc, and thus the term "employee" will be used to describe everyone in Schedule E employment.

PART I – INLAND REVENUE CONSIDERATIONS

Summary of Taxation Benefits

The taxation advantages of an exempt approved pension arrangement can be summarised simply:

a)   As far as the employer is concerned, contributions (including, subject to "clearance" by the Revenue, special lump sums) are entirely allowable as a charge against corporation tax. Thus the contributions are also deductible in calculating the required level of dividend distribution by a close company.

b)   As far as the employee is concerned, all contributions he makes, up to a maximum of 15% of remuneration, are allowable as a deduction against personal income tax liability. The contributions he makes thus reduce the marginal rate of tax on the top segment of his income.

   Furthermore, the contributions made on an employee's behalf by his employer will not be taxable on the employee as a "benefit" in kind.

   If the scheme provides for lump sum benefits payable on death in service (usually up to 4 times current salary) then such lump sums can normally be paid to the deceased's dependants free of liability to capital transfer tax.

Any pensions paid out of the scheme on a member's retirement are classified as "earned" income of the recipient, and not as investment income liable to the 15% surcharge.

A member may take part of his total pension entitlement at retirement in the form of a tax free lump sum. This can be particularly valuable for executives, since it is usually possible to receive a maximum lump sum of 1½ times final pay at retirement.

c)   As far as the fund itself is concerned, all investment income and capital gains should generally be free of tax, the only exception being that pension funds are liable for the new development land tax.

If the scheme is not "approved" by the Inland Revenue, then although the employer will normally obtain tax relief on any contributions he makes, the fund itself will not benefit from the above tax exemptions and the employee may be liable to tax as a benefit in kind in respect of employers' contributions.

Detailed Legislation

The fiscal legislation on pension schemes is supervised by the Inland Revenue Superannuation Funds Office.

The legislation governing occupational pension schemes is contained in T.A.1970 Sections 208 to 225, Finance Act 1970 Chapter 2, Part II and Schedule 5, together with Section 21 and Schedule 3 Finance Act 1971. Any scheme now established must comply with what is termed the "new code" of approval established by Finance Acts 1970 and 1971. Schemes approved by the Inland Revenue prior to that received what is termed "old code" approval, and such schemes must now be modified to comply with the new code by April 1980 at the latest. However, if an old code scheme is materially amended after April 1973 but before April 1980, then the provisions of the new code of approval must be met at the date of alteration.

The requirements which a pension scheme must meet in order to be approved by the Inland Revenue are now extremely stringent, but if a scheme does fulfil these conditions the Inland Revenue has no choice but to approve it.

However, the legislation gives the Inland Revenue discretion to approve schemes which do not exactly comply with the conditions. In consequence the Inland Revenue has issued "Practice Notes" setting out the circumstances under which schemes not complying strictly with the legislation will be approved for tax purposes.

Some of the more important features of these Practice Notes will now be described. However, since the Notes run to some 275 paragraphs (and are amended, supplemented and up-dated from time to time) what follows is obviously no more than a précis.

Employees' Contributions

Employees' contributions, up to a level of 15% of remuneration, to an approved scheme are deductible for taxation purposes. Under the present practice, employees' contributions to schemes providing only approved life assurance and/or lump sum retirement benefits will also attract full expense relief; that is to say, in order to obtain the relief contributions need not be made which will secure a pension as such.

Administrator

To secure Inland Revenue approval, an *Administrator* must be appointed for every scheme. He must be a person resident for taxation purposes in the UK.

The trustees of the scheme, or the committee of management (or in some cases the employer) would be acceptable. The Administrator is responsible for certain duties specified in the legislation, in particular:

a)   To account for any tax liability which may arise when an employee leaves service and receives a refund of his contributions during his lifetime.

b)   To account for certain returns required by the Inland Revenue.

c)   To seek approval of the scheme for tax purposes.

Limitation on Pension Benefits

To secure approval of a scheme for tax purposes there must be a limit on the benefits provided for employees.

The maximum pension which can be provided at retirement is 1/60th of final remuneration for each year of service, up to a maximum of 40 years.

There is however a concessional maximum pension which the company can provide for employees retiring with less than 40 years service with their final employer:

Years of Service to normal retirement date	Maximum Pension expressed in 60ths of final remuneration
1	1
2	2
3	3
4	4
5	5
6	8
7	16
8	24
9	32
10 or more	40

Therefore, where a person has served at least 10 years with his employer up to the normal retirement date it is *possible* (but by no means mandatory) to provide him with a pension equal to 40/60ths of his final salary. This is the maximum which can be provided.

The following points should be noted:—

a)   The term "remuneration" means basic pay for the year in question *plus* the average over a suitable period, usually 3 or more years ending on the last day of the basic pay year used, or any fluctuating emoluments. Directors' fees may be classified either as basic pay or as fluctuating emoluments, according to the basis on which they are voted.

b)   Remuneration also includes the taxable value of benefits in kind. "Final remuneration" means *either* remuneration for any 1 of the 5 years preceding the normal retirement date *or* the average of the total emoluments for any 3 or more consecutive years ending not earlier than 10 years before the normal retirement date. If a year other than that immediately before retirement is used in the calculation, the value of its remuneration for pension purposes may be increased to take into account inflation in the intervening years.

Certain restrictions are placed on the definition of final remuneration which can normally be used in the case of substantial family director/shareholders. The Inland Revenue feels that controllers of private limited companies might well give themselves a very low level of remuneration until retirement, and then pay themselves an inflated salary in the last year which would be used to calculate their approvable pension and lump-sum entitlements. The funds set aside to meet the increased pension obligations would need to be quite substantial, and of course these payments would in theory qualify for corporation tax relief. The rules therefore stipulate that controlling director/shareholders must calculate their final remuneration by reference to the average of several years and not to a single year.

c)   Where a person has served for at least 40 years, the maximum pension of 40/60ths of final salary can be given by the employer without any need to take account of "benefits" which may have arisen in respect of the previous employments of the employee.

However, increased benefits provided under a "concessional" maximum pension (see above) must take into account the value of any "retained benefits". These include any pension provided under another scheme, any self-employed annuities approved under Section 226 T.A.1970 (see Part III of this chapter), the pension equivalent of any lump sums paid or payable under previous approved schemes, and indeed certain refunds of contributions received from previous pension schemes to which the employee may have belonged. However, small deferred pensions not exceeding £52 per annum *in aggregate* may be ignored for this purpose.

Maximum Lump Sum Benefits

An Inland Revenue approved pension scheme can make a tax free lump sum payment to the retiring employee of up to 1½ times his final remuneration. Entitlement to this lump sum is calculated such that 3/80ths of final remuneration can be given for each year of service with the employer, up to a maximum of 40 years (i.e. 40 x 3/80ths = 120/80ths, or 1½).

This lump sum payable in cash and totally tax free is obviously very valuable. The higher the marginal tax rates at retirement, the more potentially attractive this entitlement becomes.

Some words of warning, however:

a)   Entitlement to a tax free lump sum payment under a pension scheme will affect the amount which can be paid as a "golden handshake"; see Chapter 8.

b)   The taking of a lump sum in this way will restrict the amount of pension which can be received. The maximum pension of up to 40/60ths of final remuneration specified above is only available if no lump sum is taken at retirement. If a lump sum is taken then the amount of pension which can be received must be reduced below the permitted maximum (see below).

As with pension entitlement, there is a "concessional" maximum lump sum for those employees who have completed less than 40 years service with their employer by the normal retirement date:

Years of Service to normal retirement age	Lump Sum expressed as 80ths of final remuneration
1	3
2	6
3	9
4	12
5	15
6	18
7	21
8	24
9	30
10	36
11	42
12	48
13	54
14	63
15	72
16	81
17	90
18	99
19	108
20 or more	120 (1½ times final remuneration)

Although any employee may be given the basic maximum lump sum benefit, the *concessional* maximum mentioned above may only be given if, when added to the value at retirement age of any "retained" lump sums, the *aggregate* does not exceed 1½ times final remuneration. Retained lump sums include those provided under a previous scheme and under Section 226 T.A.1970 annuity commutations, plus certain refunds of employee contributions under previous schemes.

Any benefit, other than a lump sum, from an approved pension scheme must be a taxable pension. The maximum approvable amount of this pension can be calculated by deducting from the maximum approvable pension (see table above) the pension "value" of the lump sum. The Inland Revenue will accept that every £9 paid in cash can mean a reduction of £1 per annum in pension, irrespective of the recipient's age and sex. Alternatively, where pension is commuted to provide the lump sum a table of conversion factors taking into account age and sex would be considered by the Inland Revenue.

Examples

1.   Bert Pritchard has worked with his employer for 45 years and has reached the retirement age of 65. His final salary is £3,000 a year.

      On the Inland Revenue approved basis, the maximum permissible pension which the company can pay Bert is £2,000 a year (i.e. 2/3rds of £3,000), and the maximum lump sum he can receive tax free is £4,500 (1½ times final remuneration).

2.   Bert cannot take both a pension of £2,000 per annum *and* a tax free lump sum of £4,500. If he wants the lump sum, then the amount of pension payable to him must be reduced.

      The amount of the reduction in pension can be ascertained either by reference to some approved factor, or on the basis of a £1 reduction in pension for every £9 of tax free lump sum. Using this latter basis, this means that by taking a £4,500 tax free lump sum Bert's maximum pension will be reduced from £2,000 to £1,500 per annum.

3.   Sylvia Evans has completed only 15 years' service with her employer and she is now retiring at the age of 60. Her final salary is also £3,000.

      Since Sylvia has completed more than 10 years' service, her employer can still give her an Inland Revenue approved maximum pension of 2/3rds of her final salary; that is to say, a pension of £2,000 per annum, similar to Bert's.

However, since Sylvia has completed only 15 years' service, she cannot receive full entitlement to the lump sum. The above table shows that her maximum entitlement to a tax free lump sum is 72/80ths of final remuneration, that is, £2,700. If she does decide to take this amount, her pension of £2,000 per annum maximum must be reduced accordingly.

Therefore it is now possible to establish a "pension scheme" fully approved by the Superannuation Funds Office which provides only cash benefits up to the appropriate maximum for the individual concerned. There is no obligation for employers to provide a pension with the cash benefits.

Life Assurance Benefits on Death in Service

For schemes approved under the new code, the maximum death in service (as opposed to death after retirement) benefit payable is 4 times the employee's current remuneration. This lump sum payment is quite distinct from any return of employee's contributions which may be made on his death.

This lump sum life assurance benefit is normally payable to the deceased's dependants totally free of capital transfer tax.

The Inland Revenue has issued a press release to "answer enquiries about the capital transfer tax liability of benefits payable under pension schemes". This confirms that no capital transfer tax liability will arise in respect of benefits payable on a person's death under a normal pension scheme, unless:

a)   The benefits form part of the deceased's freely disposable property passing under his Will or intestacy. This applies only if his executors or administrators have a legally enforceable claim to the benefits; if the benefits are payable to them only at the discretion of the trustees of the pension fund (or some similar person) they are not liable to capital transfer tax,

or b)   the deceased had the power immediately before his death to nominate or appoint the benefit to anyone he pleased.

Death in Service — Pension Benefits

A pension scheme may also provide some form of widow's or dependants' pension should the employee die before retirement. The term
dependant means a child of the employee who is either under the age
of 18 or receiving full time education *or* any person who is genuinely
financially dependent on the employee.

The pension which can be provided is equal to 2/3rds of the
member's maximum approvable pension, calculated as if he had survived
until normal retirement age but with no change in his remuneration.

Where there are both dependants *and* a widow, separate pensions can
be provided for all or any of them up to the 2/3rds limitation, but the
aggregate of widow's plus dependants' pensions must not exceed what
would have been the member's maximum approvable pension calculated
had he survived to normal retirement age.

Again, in determining the value of lump sum and pension benefits
the company may provide on death during service, account must be
taken of any other benefits to which the employee may remain entitled
as a result of previous employments, although "trivial" amounts can be
ignored.

Early Retirement

Benefits may be provided if a member of a pension scheme is obliged to
retire early, before the normal retirement age of the scheme. If however
the retirement is *not* owing to incapacity, then an *immediate benefit*
may only be paid if retirement occurs after the age of 50.

Working After Retirement

An employee who continues in the employment after normal retirement
age may qualify for additional benefits.

Firstly, pensions (including the pension value of any benefit taken
in lump sum form) may be calculated by taking the actual date of
retirement as the normal retirement date, so that when calculating the
concessional maximum pension, final remuneration at the *actual* date

of retirement and all years of service can be counted. If the total service exceeds 40 years, each year of service after the normal retirement age may earn further "60ths of final remuneration" at the actual date of retirement. The maximum number of years permissible is 45, producing a maximum pension of 45/60ths of final remuneration.

Alternatively, the pension payable from the member's true normal retirement age may be increased actuarily.

Lump sums can be similarly increased. This may be calculated either by years of service — the maximum permissible number of years is again 45, producing a maximum lump sum of 135/80ths of final remuneration — or alternatively the lump sum payable at the normal retirement age may be increased by interest at a rate similar to the rate earned on the scheme's assets.

Inflation after Retirement

Pensions actually being paid may be increased during retirement to keep pace with inflation. Indeed, it is possible to fund in advance for inflation, provided that the estimated rate of increase is "reasonable" and that the rules of the scheme provide for the proper disposal of any surplus which may result from an over-estimate of the rate of increase.

Death After Retirement

The widow's or dependants' pension which may be provided follows the same pattern as that described for death in service.

Lump sum payments, other than guarantees of pension for a minimum term, are treated by the Inland Revenue as further lump sum retirement benefits and must be calculated accordingly. Also, with one exception, life assurance cover must be paid to the deceased's legal personal representatives.

Equal Access

Under the new code of approval, an employer may establish a pension scheme for one employee only. Certain employees may well benefit from a pensions package tailored to their individual situation. If a pension scheme is to be open to employees generally, or to a specific sector of employees, this is quite acceptable.

From April 1978 it is *not permissible* to deny participation in a pension scheme to women with the same job classification as the male employees who are eligible. This also applies where Inland Revenue approval is not being sought. Nevertheless, it is permissible (at least for the moment) to discriminate concerning the benefits provided, and thus while women must be given equal access to the scheme, they need not be given identical or equal benefits under it.

Leaving Service

The legislation dealing with preservation of pensions insists in most cases on an employee's right to a deferred pension (including any dependants' benefits) on leaving service. Refunds of employees' contributions are normally only available if the employee has been a member of the scheme for less than 5 years.

The option of a refund of contributions is only restricted for those employees whose earnings have exceeded £5,000 (in any year) where contributions were being made before 6th April 1975.

PART II – STATE SCHEME CONSIDERATIONS

Introduction

From 6th April 1978 quite dramatic changes will be made in the present State pension scheme. This new scheme, popularly termed the "Castle Scheme" after its instigator Barbara Castle, formerly Secretary of State for Social Security, is the third major attempt in the last decade to provide reasonable old age pensions for the whole community and at the same time to introduce acceptable compromises between pensions provided by the State and those provided by privately-administered pension funds. Unlike the previous Crossman and Joseph proposals, the Castle Scheme has apparently been accepted by all major political parties and it therefore seems unlikely that the proposals will be abolished (although they may well be modified) should a change of government occur.

An Outline of the Scheme

The object of the Castle Scheme, or to give it its precise title, the Social Security Pensions Act 1975, is to ensure that all employees are entitled to a "reasonable" pension from the State commencing at retirement age, which is 65 for men and 60 for women.

The retirement pension will be made up from two distinct sources: —

i)   Firstly there will be a basic flat rate of State pension regardless of salary or income level.

ii)   In addition to the basic State pension, there will be an earnings-related pension, popularly known as the "Additional Pension".

The amount of this additional pension depends on the employee's earnings over a period of up to 20 years: 1.25% of "qualifying earnings" will be taken each year, so that after 20 years the additional pension will be equal to the maximum entitlement of 25% of qualifying earnings.

These qualifying earnings may equally well be described as "upper band earnings". They are ascertained by taking as the lower level an amount approximately equal to a single person's State pension and taking as the upper level 7 times this figure. At the rates in force at mid-1977, the lower level for qualifying earnings is £15 and the upper level is £105 (i.e. 7 x £15).

Example

Let us assume, somewhat unrealistically, that there will be no inflation during the next 20 years and no increase in the basic State pensions. Ken Wood of Car-County Insurance Company Limited earns £31 a week and contributes fully to the State Scheme between 1978 and 1998, his 65th birthday. His total final pension will therefore be:

    i)   £15.30

plus ii)   1.25% of his upper band earnings (i.e. £31 − £15) x
20 years qualifying service = 1.25% of £16 x 20 = £4.

Ken's total State pension is therefore £15.30 + £4 = £19.30.
Since his income is £31 a week, he will retire on a pension substantially more than half-pay.

Additional Calculations

The above example is expressed in the simplest terms and makes no
allowance for inflation. The following complications should therefore
be borne in mind:

i)   The "upper band earnings" will be reviewed each April to keep
pace with inflation. If in 1979 the lower level is increased to say
£20 a week, the upper band earnings will then be between £20
and £140 a week.

ii)   Only an employee who works for a complete 20 years after April
1978 will be entitled to receive the full pension of 25% of the
upper band earnings. A taxpayer who retires in say 1988 will
only be entitled to a pension of 1.25% x 10 = 12.50% of upper
band earnings.

iii) Although the additional pension is based on upper band earnings,
the earnings themselves will be re-valued every year. Therefore,
if an employee retires in 1998, having completed 20 years'
service, the 25% extra pension will be based on his re-valued
annual earnings for each year of membership, not his actual
earnings during that period.
    This re-valuation will be calculated by reference to an index
of national average earnings.

iv) Where a person works for *more* than 20 years after 1978, the
additional pension will be based on 1.25% of his re-valued earnings
for the "best" 20 years of membership.

v)   The additional pension will be increased *during payment*, to keep
     abreast with the movement of retail prices. The basic State
     pension is of course normally increased in accordance with the
     movement of national average earnings.

Widow's Pension

The State will also provide a widow's and invalidity pension in two
parts — basic and additional — calculated in much the same way as the
retirement pension. Briefly, where a husband dies after retirement at
age 65 his widow will receive her deceased husband's full additional
pension, as well as any earned in her own right. However, if the husband
dies before retirement, the widow would normally only receive her late
husband's full additional pension earned to date if *she* is then over age
50.

A widower will be entitled to any pension earned by his deceased
spouse *only if* they are both past retirement age at the relevant time.

National Insurance Contributions

Although the actual level of contributions will obviously depend on the
financial climate in 1978 and the number of those who decide to
"contract out" (see below), it is presently envisaged that the rate of
contributions for employees will be 6½% per annum and for employers
10% per annum. Clearly this rate will only apply to the range of
earnings up to the then "contribution ceiling" which is equivalent to
the top limit of the upper earnings band, above which no contributions
are payable either by the employee or the employer.

The 2% increase in employers' national insurance contributions
announced several months ago is not included in the above figures,
since it is in effect a payroll tax (as opposed to a national insurance
contribution), and it is paid directly to the Exchequer rather than to
the National Insurance Fund.

Disadvantages of the State Scheme

Although the new State scheme will provide larger pensions than before,
it is still in many ways inadequate as compared with a good occupational pension scheme.

a)   The earnings-related pension benefit only applies up to the upper level of national insurance contributions. Consequently, executives will earn no additional pension entitlement beyond this level, and the eventual State pension will only amount to a modest proportion of the executive's final salary at retirement.

b)   The State scheme provides inadequate widows' pensions, particularly for young widows.

c)   There is no lump sum death benefit before retirement (i.e. no sum equalling 4 times remuneration, as explained in Part I).

d)   There is no lump sum tax free benefit on retirement (i.e. no sum equalling 1½ times final remuneration, as explained in Part I).

e)   Employees' contributions to the State scheme do not qualify for income tax relief.

f)   The State scheme is inflexible and cannot be adapted to meet the requirements of individual companies. A good example of this is the absence of provisions in the State scheme for the early retirement of employees.

g)   The State scheme is run on a "pay-as-you-go" basis, with no advance funding of liability. Future benefits therefore depend on the willingness of the next generation of working people to maintain the required level of contributions.

Contracting Out

Provided the Occupational Pensions Board (a body set up to control and administer non-fiscal aspects of pension schemes) is satisfied that a privately run company pension scheme is set up properly, has adequate financial resources, and is subject to regular financial scrutiny, and provided the pension scheme ensures a reasonable level of benefit, such a company scheme may be used to "contract out" employees from part of the State scheme.

It is not possible to contract out of the *basic* old age pension.

However, private schemes satisfying the above conditions may contract out employees from the obligation to provide additional pensions via the State.

Where a scheme is contracted out, both the employer and the employee will pay less in contributions to the State. Assuming that the figures mentioned above (6½% for employees and 10% for employers) are correct for 1978, it is envisaged that the employees' contributions will be reduced to 4% and the employers' contributions to 5½%. Thus there is a total saving of 7% in respect of contributions which would otherwise have been paid to the National Insurance Fund, a saving split 4½% in favour of the employer and 2½% to the employee.

Since it is only possible to contract out of the additional pension, the reduced contributions relate to the upper earnings band and *not* to earnings below this level (presently £15 per week).

Example

> If an employee presently earns £30 a week, it is envisaged that from April 1978 the employer will pay a national insurance contribution of 10% (£3) per week and the employee will pay 6½% (£1.95) per week. Should the employee be contracted out of the additional pension, then the contribution levels in respect of the first £15 will be 10% and 6½% respectively, but the contributions on the next £15 will be 5½% (82½p) for the employer and 4% (60p) for the employee.

The 7% difference in national insurance contributions between contracting out and contracting in will apply from April 1978, regardless of the actual level of national insurance contributions set at that time. However, the Government actuary has predicted that this difference will diminish by one-half a per cent every 5 years, until in 25 years time it will be only 4½%.

Contracting Out Terms

Before a company scheme can be contracted out of the additional State pension scheme, the Occupational Pensions Board must be satisfied that it has been established with adequate financial resources and controls. In practice this means that the scheme must either be underwritten by a life assurance company or, if self invested, must receive regular Certificates of Solvency from a qualified actuary. In addition, the contracted out scheme must provide a minimum level of benefits, so that the employee at least receives as much as he would have done under the State scheme. The main conditions which have to be met before a private pension scheme can be contracted out are:

a)   The scheme must guarantee a benefit of at least 1/80th of "final salary" for each year of future membership. An index linked average salary may be used instead of final salary.

There are several acceptable definitions of final salary. The member's earnings up to 1½ times the lower level of upper band earnings could be excluded, since these can be regarded as covered by the basic State pension. For example, if an employee is earning £65 a week and the basic State pension is £15 a week, then the definition of final salary may be £42.50 a week (i.e. £65 − (£15 x 1½) = £65 − £22.50 = £42.50).

There is no obligation to provide pensions for years of service prior to April 1978.

b)   The contracted out scheme must provide a widow's pension on death before retirement and also on death after retirement. The scale must be at least one one hundred and sixtieth (1/160th) of "final salary" for each year of membership. Strictly speaking, for a scheme to satisfy the contracting out requirements, the widow's benefits need therefore only relate to *accrued* years of membership rather than *prospective* years of membership.

c)   The contracted out scheme must provide for the accrual of a Guaranteed Minimum Pension (GMP). This is a pension approximately equal to the additional pension which the member might have been accruing had he been contracted into the State scheme. A widow's GMP, at 50% of GMP, must also be provided. However, any increases in GMP after retirement will be the responsibility of the State scheme, not the private scheme.

d) Employees leaving service before retirement with at least 5 years contracted out membership must have preserved for them a pension at a rate not less than the GMP (although of course it can be more). The GMP portion of the preserved contracted out pension must be increased during deferment by one of the following three methods:—

    i)   Revaluing the GMP to keep abreast of average earnings.

    ii)   Increasing the GMP by 5% per annum, *and* paying over an amount to the State scheme which will cover any excess over the 5%,

or iii) The occupational scheme undertaking to provide an increasing GMP at a fixed rate of 8½% per annum.

Where schemes have used methods (i) and (ii) above but fall short of (i), the State system provides the balance required.

Whichever of the above methods is chosen, it must apply to everyone who leaves service, although the method may be changed later in respect of future leavers.

Where a member leaves service with less than 5 years contracted out membership, the contracted out scheme may generally make a lump sum payment into the State scheme equal to the contributions which would have been paid had the employee *not* been contracted out, as an alternative to preserving the benefits within the occupational scheme itself. This lump sum payment does *not* carry interest against the company to compensate for the fact that the Government could have invested those funds had they been paid on the due dates.

Decision Day

Whether or not to contract out of the State scheme is a difficult decision, and no simple financial comparison can automatically indicate the right course of action. However, the decision is not irrevocable, and most companies will probably review the situation at 5-yearly intervals, when the contribution terms for contracting out are themselves reviewed by the Government.

Although contracted out status does have a number of advantages, such as increased flexibility, tax relief on employees' contributions, more advantageous lump sum benefits etc, these must be weighed against the greater financial risks which contracting out might involve, particularly in relation to the benefits which have to be provided for employees who leave service before retirement. Of course, the advantages of a good private pension scheme could be preserved by providing it as an *addition to* contracting into the State scheme, without in any way having to reduce the benefits under the private scheme.

Some employers are indeed opting for this middle course, of contracting into the State scheme but also providing benefits from their own private scheme in addition to the State benefits. These additional benefits are intended to rectify defects in the State scheme, and would typically include substantial death in service cover, tax free lump sums on retirement, and so on.

Time is now short. A substantial backlog of applications to contract out could well have built up by 6th April 1978, and the Occupational Pensions Board may be unable to give a decision on the status of a particular scheme by that date. Thus an employer may find himself involuntarily contracted in for a few months, until the Occupational Pensions Board Certificate is received. Furthermore, a company must notify its employees by December 1977 whether or not it intends to contract out of the additional pension. Before then, considerable staff consultation will have to take place, since it is a legal requirement to confer with recognised trade unions about the decision to contract in or out.

PART III — SELF EMPLOYED

A self employed (Schedule D) taxpayer must make his own arrangements for pension entitlement, since he cannot do so within an employer's scheme as described in Part I of this chapter. People who work for self employed taxpayers, and therefore pay tax under Schedule E, may of course participate in a group scheme, but the proprietor or partners cannot.

Technically, anyone who is not in pensionable employment may take advantage of what are termed self employed retirement annuities. Although these usually concern the Schedule D taxpayer, the benefits of such provisions are also available to Schedule E taxpayers who for some reason do not participate in an employer's group scheme. For example, an employer may not wish to run a private pension fund, or if he does, the employee might not be eligible to join. Indeed, some employees do not care to join their employer's scheme, even though they are entitled to do so.

Therefore, these retirement annuities must be discussed in relation to any person who does not have pensionable employment; they cannot simply be termed "self employed annuities".

Basic Advantages

Since the 1956 Finance Act self employed taxpayers and employees in non-pensionable employment have been able to set aside part of their earnings each year to secure a pension during retirement, and such sums have been deductible from their income tax liability.

The advantages of this arrangement are:

a)   Provided they fall within the qualifying limits specified below, the contributions set aside are deductible for income tax at both basic and higher rates. They are *not* deductible in calculating the investment income surcharge.

b)   The investment fund into which the contributions are paid is not liable to tax on its income or its capital profits (although it is liable to the new development land tax).

c)   Any pension which emerges at retirement is classified as earned as opposed to investment income, and it is now possible to *commute* part of this pension entitlement for a tax free lump sum.

Amount of Tax Deductible Contributions

The amount of tax deductible contributions available within this category is generally less than can be provided under a pension scheme sponsored by an employer. Quite apart from the fact that the taxpayer making his own pension arrangements will not receive the tax free benefit of employers' contributions, the amount which the individual can set aside, particularly the highly-paid executive, is less than under an employer-sponsored scheme.

The amount of tax deductible contributions is fixed by reference to the *lower* of two sums: a specified figure, and a percentage of what are termed "net relevant earnings".

The term "net relevant earnings" is explained in the next section. From time to time the amount of such tax deductible contributions is increased to keep pace with inflation. The 1977 Finance Act provided that, for taxpayers born after 1915, the amount of tax deductible contribution is the *lower* of £3,000 and 15% of the net relevant earnings, and for taxpayers born prior to 1916, the amount is as follows:

	Allowable Contribution, being the smaller of:	
Year of Birth	Amount	Net relevant earnings
	£	%
1914/1915	3,600	18
1912/1913	4,200	21
1910/1911	4,800	24
1908/1909	5,400	27
1907 or earlier	6,000	30

Net Relevant Earnings

The term "net relevant earnings" basically means income either from a non-pensionable employment or from self employed activities. Thus non-pensionable Schedule E income and Schedule D Case I and II income would normally qualify. However, certain other income such as Schedule A income from land, Schedule B income from woodlands, and income derived from patents may also qualify.

The following points should also be noted:

i)   A wife's income is to be determined quite independently of her
     husband's.

ii) Certain Schedule E income from "controlled" investment com-
     panies cannot be taken into account; unusually, no such problems
     arise in relation to employer-sponsored pension schemes.

iii) In calculating net relevant earnings, any items which are allowable
     for taxation purposes must be deducted and any losses incurred
     by the trade or business must also be taken into account.

Widows' and Dependants' Benefits

Where a taxpayer has wished to ensure that his widow or dependants
will receive a pension which continues after his death, he has always
been able to allocate part of his pension entitlement to this purpose
and take a reduced pension himself.

However, some years ago the tax relief on self employed annuities
was amended so that a taxpayer may now contribute a specified proportion of his tax deductible contribution towards some form of lump
sum life cover or some form of pension for his widow or dependants.
The 1977 Finance Act has increased the allowable contribution to the
lower of £1,000 per annum or 5% of net relevant earnings. This allowance is not *in addition to* those set out above, but is part of them. For
example, if a 35 year old taxpayer making the maximum contribution
of £3,000 per annum wishes to secure substantial widow's or dependants' benefits, he may pay up to £1,000 towards such provision, but
the tax deductible contribution in respect of his own pension entitlement is reduced to a maximum of £2,000.

Therefore, the taxpayer contributing towards a lump sum death
benefit will be entitled to claim relief as a tax deductible expense. These
are much more advantageous terms than are applicable to life assurance
policies, which only qualify for tax relief at one-half of the basic rate.
At present therefore, relief on policy premiums is 17%, in contrast with
the potential relief of 83% available under a self employed annuity type
of life assurance benefit. One drawback to life cover of this kind,
however, is that the proceeds must be payable to the deceased's estate

and are thus potentially liable to capital transfer tax, unless the entire estate is left to the surviving spouse. In contrast, the life assurance death in service benefit provided under employer-sponsored schemes will almost invariably be free of capital transfer tax.

Necessary Conditions for Approval

Before a self employed annuity policy is entitled to the taxation benefits described above, the following conditions must be met (quite apart from the contribution limitations):

i)   The contributions must be paid by the taxpayer to secure an annuity which commences not earlier than the age of 60 but not later than the age of 75.

ii) Despite condition (i), the annuity *may* commence before the age of 60 *either* if the taxpayer is obliged to retire early because of infirmity of body or mind *or* it is CUSTOMARY in that taxpayer's particular employment, trade or profession to retire before the age of 60. In the latter case, the annuity may commence at any time after the age of 50.

iii) The annuity secured by the taxpayer's contributions is not capable of being assigned, surrendered or commuted in whole or in part.
   The one exception to this rule relates to commutation. The taxpayer may now take part of his pension entitlement at retirement in the form of a lump sum, in much the same way as under an employer-sponsored scheme. However, the lump sum taken must not exceed 3 times the annual amount of the remaining annuity.

Example

Taxpayer A wishes to commute part of his pension entitlement for £14,500, leaving himself a reduced pension of £5,000 per annum. This is permissible.
   Taxpayer B wishes to take £16,000 cash, and a pension of

£5,000 payable for life. This is *not* permissible: the maximum amount which may be taken in cash is £15,000, since this is 3 times the annual value of the remaining pension.

iv)   Where contributions are paid to secure a lump sum on death or an annuity for a widow or dependant, any *lump sum* payable on death must be payable to the taxpayer's personal representatives and cannot be paid as such directly to a beneficiary or a dependant.

Contracting Out

In Part II of this chapter, the contracting out rules were described.

Unfortunately, only employer sponsored schemes (described in Part I) may be used for contracting out of the State Scheme and it is not possible for employed taxpayers with "self employed" annuities to be contracted out.

PART IV — OVERSEAS ASPECTS

The following points are of importance.

Effect of 1977 Finance Act Provisions

As was explained in Chapter 9 UK taxpayers with overseas sources of income may be entitled to either a 100% or a 25% deduction (depending on the circumstances) in computing their UK tax liability.

The effect of such tax benefits on an employer sponsored pension scheme (as described in Part I of this chapter) appears to be as follows:

1.   UK Resident employer

If the employer is a UK resident for tax purposes then all employees may be provided with benefits under a UK approved scheme in respect of their service with the company *regardless of* whether or not they are chargeable to income tax. Thus, taking an extreme case, an employee who qualifies for the 100% deduction, and therefore has no UK tax liability for emoluments receivable from the company, is quite free to receive the maximum approvable pension benefits in the UK.

Likewise, if the employee is entitled to the 25% deduction only, then his UK pension entitlement can still be based on 100% of his emoluments, even though he or she may only be taxable on 75% of his emoluments.

2.   Employer not Resident in the UK

If the employer is an overseas employer — that is to say one not resident in the UK for tax purposes — employees may only take part in a UK approved pension scheme when they are termed "effectively chargeable" to UK income tax under either Schedule E Case I or Schedule E Case II.

This means that employees qualifying for the 100% deduction cannot join a UK approved scheme. However, employees entitled to the 25% deduction can join in respect of 100% of their emoluments, because they are "effectively chargeable" to UK tax.

A further complication for pension purposes in respect of an employment with an overseas employer is that only the years in which the employee is "effectively chargeable" to UK tax can count as qualifying years of service.

Overseas Pension Schemes

Where a UK taxpayer is entitled to participate in a pension scheme established outside the UK tax jurisdiction, the question raised (quite apart from any overseas taxation considerations) is whether or not the benefit of the scheme ought to be taxable as a benefit in kind (in accordance with Section 23 F.A.1970).

In all cases the Superannuation Funds Office will need to see copies of the scheme rules and related documentation. Provided the scheme does not secure benefits in excess of the maximum approvable under the UK legislation and that a person resident in the UK is appointed to act for the Administrator, then the employer's contributions will not rank as a taxable benefit in kind. However, if the overseas pension scheme provides benefits widely out of line with the maximum approvable benefits under a UK scheme, the Inland Revenue will take the view that the employee should be taxable on all of this employer's payment as a benefit in kind subject to the 100% or 25% deductions applicable to the overseas emoluments.

Retirement

i)   If a UK taxpayer decides to retire overseas, he may be entitled to receive a pension from a UK employer. The basic rule is that income tax under the PAYE system must be deducted at source by the Trustee of the pension fund or by the employer paying the annuity.

      However, as most UK double taxation treaties provide that pension entitlements are only taxable in the country of *residence*, permission will usually be obtained from the UK authorities to pay the pension without tax deduction to an overseas pensioner.

ii)   Where a UK national is transferred to another country in circumstances such that he may well retire in that overseas country, the question sometimes occurs as to whether the liability to make pension payments may be transferred from the UK employer to the overseas employer. The UK employer may wish to make a lump sum payment to the overseas employer as a recompense for him taking over the UK employer's accrued pension liabilities.

      In these circumstances, it must be ensured that the scheme rules enable a payment of this nature to be made and that the transfer is made in accordance with Bank of England exchange control regulations.

      The attitude of the Superannuation Funds Office is that a transfer payment of this nature to an overseas pension scheme can only be made where — so far as can be seen at the time — the member has been transferred to overseas service on a *permanent* basis. They will also want to be satisfied as to the standing of the new employer if the employment is not a public office or with the same group as the UK employer. If so, the general requirement is that the transfer payment to the overseas scheme can only be taken in pension form by the employee. This restriction applies in nearly all circumstances, including leaving service before normal retirement age as well as on actual retirement. The only exception is that lump sum payments can be made should the employee die during service. (Any requirements of the Occupational Pensions Board concerning contracting out and the preservation of pension rights will also need to be observed where the service terminates before normal retirement date).

Before giving approval, the Superannuation Funds Office will need to see certified copies of the full overseas documentation governing the new pension scheme. Undertakings will usually be required from the overseas pension scheme along the lines indicated above.

iii) Where a UK taxpayer retires in the UK after overseas service he may be entitled to receive a pension from one or more overseas employers.

The tax position of such pensions payable from overseas is governed by Section 22 F.A.1974, which provides that 10% of the pension entitlement is tax free and the remaining 90% is taxable in the ordinary way by reference to the pension entitlement *arising* in the fiscal year.

CHAPTER 11

SOCIAL SECURITY – THE COSTS AND BENEFITS

The legislation dealing with the UK's social security system is complex. The overall system is run by the Department of Health and Social Security whose main offices are at Alexander Fleming House, Elephant and Castle, London SE1, telephone 01 407 5522.

The range of ·benefits commences with the maternity grant and ends with the death grant. In the intervening period a variety of benefits are given, amongst which are:

a)   Unemployment.

b)   Sickness.

c)   Invalidity.

d)   Widows' allowances and pensions

e)   Retirement pensions (see previous chapter)

f)   Children's special allowances

Thus the range of potential benefits is extremely wide. There is usually a requirement to have a certair. amount of contributions paid over a minimum period of time, and to be present in the UK at the time the benefit is claimed. However, the actual conditions to be met in any particular case depend upon the allowance, grant or benefit which is being claimed and thus each benefit needs to be examined separately to see whether the claim is likely to succeed.

Surprisingly little has been written about national insurance. One major reason is perhaps the frequent changes in the contributions required and in the benefits received. This chapter will therefore explain certain aspects of the overall system which may be of particular interest to readers. Anyone wishing to know more about a specific point should contact their local Department of Health and Social Security office for up-to-date information on the benefit in question. Appendix I to this chapter is a comprehensive list of the main DHSS information leaflets currently available. Since contribution rates and benefits provided are constantly changing, Appendix II summarises the main contributions and benefits in force at the time of going to press.

History

The first national insurance scheme covering health and unemployment benefit was introduced by the National Insurance Act in 1911. By that time certain friendly societies, trade unions and industrial societies were already running health insurance schemes. These "approved societies" were now entrusted with administering the health scheme on the Government's behalf, whilst the unemployment benefit scheme was run by the then Ministry of Labour through the employment exchanges.

Over the years dramatic changes took place, and Sir William Beveridge was eventually appointed to review the entire system of State insurance and State benefits. His report, published in 1942, led to the National Insurance Act 1946, the Act upon which the structure of the present welfare state is based.

Contributions

The welfare system is largely financed by contributions from the working population. There are four distinct classes of contribution:

Class 1: This relates to Schedule E taxpayers, and consists of

      a)   primary contributions paid by all "earners" (i.e. employees and office holders),

and b)   secondary contributions paid by employers.

      Class 1 contributions are earnings-related, that is, based on a specified percentage of the taxpayer's emoluments.

Class 2: These contributions are paid by the self-employed (Schedule D taxpayers). Contributions are payable weekly at a flat rate, and are not earnings-related.

Class 3: These contributions, also payable weekly at a flat rate, are voluntary. They are paid by taxpayers in order to secure (or indeed to make up a certain entitlement to) various benefits, the most important being retirement pensions.

Class 4: These contributions are earnings-related, and are paid by the self employed in respect of profits or gains of a trade, profession or vocation taxable under Schedule D Cases I or II.

Therefore, anyone who is employed pays earnings-related contributions under Class 1, and his employer also pays contributions under Class 1. Earnings-related contributions are not payable above a certain ceiling (see Appendix II).

The self employed pay Class 2 contributions plus, if their income exceeds a fairly modest level, Class 4 contributions. Class 2 contributions are flat rate, whereas Class 4 are earnings-related, once again up to a certain level.

It should normally be clear whether a person is an "employee" or "self employed" for the purpose of ascertaining which class of contributions he ought to pay. Company directors for example pay Class 1 contributions, but prior to 6th April 1975 they were regarded as self employed and thus paid Class 2 contributions. At the moment a minister of religion is regarded as self employed and hence is liable to Class 2 and 4 contributions, but it has recently been announced that they will be designated "employed" in the future. Certain self employed people who are supplied through agencies (e.g. temporary secretaries) are classified as contributors under Class 1 rather than Class 2 and 4.

Employees (Class 1)

Social security contributions paid by Class 1 contributors are collected by the employer under the general PAYE system. The old system of cards with stamps affixed to them has been abolished and all records of both taxation and social security payments are kept on the PAYE deduction cards.

In general, the liability to make contributions, for both the employee and the employer, commences with any payment of earnings made to an employee from the date on which he reaches the minimum school leaving age, normally 16, even though the employee may still be at school (i.e. working during school holidays) and irrespective of whether the pay in question was earned before or after that date. There is no liability on the employer or employee to make contributions arising from payments made before the school leaving age.

At the other end of the scale, if the employee is over the minimum pensionable age, 65 for a man and 60 for a woman, and is retired from regular employment, he or she does not have to pay national insurance contributions on any payment received from an employer. However, both the employer and employee must pay earnings-related Class 1 contributions, and therefore if an employer takes on a pensioner the employer is still liable to pay full national insurance contributions.

The national insurance contributions are based on the gross pay of the employee, including overtime pay, commissions, salaries, holiday pay, gratuities and so on. However, items such as benefits in kind are not taken into account. Therefore, if an executive is paid predominantly in benefits in kind, then both his and his employer's liability to national insurance contributions will be based solely on the cash emoluments, and not the benefits in kind, even though these benefits in kind may be liable to tax.

An employee may have more than one employment; if so, full Class 1 contributions must be paid by the employee, and each employer, on the earnings from each employment. However, the employee cannot pay contributions in excess of those payable on the upper earnings limit, presently £105 a week. If his total employment incomes exceed this figure he will be entitled to a refund of overpaid contributions. Such cases should be notified to the Department of Health and Social Security, who will send an application form for a refund to the employee after the end of the contribution year. Unfortunately, no such provision applies to employers, and they are unable to reclaim contributions from the Department of Health and Social Security.

Example

Elio Ducati has separate employment contracts with the following companies:

Velocette Investments
Douglas International
Norton Trading

Mr. Ducati receives £100 a week from each company.

Mr. Ducati and his 3 employers must each pay their ordinary weekly contributions, which means that in all three cases Mr. Ducati will pay £5.75 a week and the employers will *each* pay £10.75.

At the end of the year Mr. Ducati will have paid his 5.75% contribution on a total of £300 a week, whereas the upper earnings limit is £105 a week. Therefore he will be entitled to reclaim the contributions paid on the surplus £195 from the Department of Health and Social Security. However, the three employers, who each paid £10.75 a week, are not entitled to a refund.

In certain circumstances, payment of the *employee's* primary contributions may be deferred if he is liable to pay Class 1 contributions on two or more employments and expects to pay contributions on one of them on or above the upper earnings limit (as specified in Appendix II) throughout the year. If the employer obtains deferment, a certificate to this effect will be issued by the Department of Health and Social Security to the employer, instructing him not to deduct contributions in the appropriate circumstances.

Company Directors

As a general rule, Class 1 contributions are payable by a director (and his company) in respect of each separately remunerated directorship or employment. This liability is not affected by the way in which the Inland Revenue may collect income tax on these emoluments. As explained above, although the director may obtain a refund if his total contributions exceed those applicable to the upper earnings limit, no such refund is available to the employers.

There are however two exceptions to this rule:

i)   Where an individual holds directorships or employments in a number of associated companies within a group *but* his total remuneration is paid by *only one of them*. In this situation national insurance contributions are calculated on the single payment in precisely the same way as if only one company employer were involved. The individual and his companies are not required to make multiple contributions, and there will therefore be no excess contributions to be refunded subsequently.

ii) Where a director has been appointed as the *nominee* of another company, contributions are not payable on the emoluments of that directorship provided that:

a)   The principal company has the right to appoint directors to the Board of the other company by virtue of its shareholding in (or other form of agreement with) the secondary company,

and b)   the director is required to surrender his fees to the nominating company, such that the Inland Revenue regards the income handed over as being that of the nominating company and not of that of the director personally.

A professional person such as an accountant or solicitor, employed on his own account or in partnership, may often be appointed to the Board of a client company for his professional services. If the fees are shown in the company's records as being voted or payable to the director BY NAME there will be a liability for Class 1 contributions. This is so regardless of whether the fees are paid to the director personally, or made over to his firm to be redistributed as profits, or in the case of a partnership shared according to the formula set out in the Deed of Partnership.

Earnings Period

As a general rule, Case I contributions are due at the time the earnings are paid. Thus if earnings are paid weekly, insurance contributions will be due weekly, and so on. Special rules apply to employees without regular employment, such as part-time gardeners.

The earnings period (i.e. the interval between payments) is important, not only for determining the date of liability but also its amount; see the calculation of the upper earnings limit described in Appendix II. If a person receives his earnings at two or more regular intervals, the earnings period is the shorter of the two intervals; if the interval is less than 7 days, the earnings period will be a week. However, if the *greatest* part of a person's earnings is normally paid at intervals longer than the shortest pay interval, the Secretary of State for Health and Social Services may in certain circumstances direct that the earnings period shall thereafter be based on some interval other than the shortest regular pay interval; both the employee and the employer will be notified accordingly.

This principle is best illustrated by an example. An extreme case has been chosen, but it must be stressed that if the Secretary of State decides that earnings are being paid in such a way that Class 1 contributions are being avoided or reduced by means of irregular or unequal payments, then he may direct that the contributions be paid to the Department of Health and Social Security as if the practice of irregular and unequal payments were not being followed.

Example

John Wurzel works for Automatic Corn Planting Company Ltd. and is paid £20 a week. However, at the end of the year he receives a bonus of £5,000, so in that last week he effectively earns £5,020.

For each week except the last, both the employee and the employer will pay their respective Class 1 contributions (primary and secondary) by reference to an income of £20. In the last week Mr. Wurzel will pay his contribution of 5.75% based on the upper earnings limit of £105 *for that week*, and likewise the employer will pay his contribution of 10.75% on the maximum of £105.

The payments in excess of this figure will not be liable to further contributions. Had the bonus been spread throughout the year, as part of Mr. Wurzel's salary, contributions *each week* would have been ascertained by reference to £105, and thus the contributions paid by the employee and employer would have been some five times greater.

Complications can arise in the case of company directors, many of whom are voted the bulk of their remuneration at yearly intervals. They are thus best assessed for contribution liability on an *annual* earnings period, instead of following the normal rules. For instance, if a director receives a salary of £200 a month and an annual bonus of £2,450, the Secretary of State may direct that the earnings period will be a year rather than, as normally, a month.

Married Women Employees

In the past, married women and certain widows could opt to pay a reduced primary Class 1 contribution of only 2% of their pay. Despite this, the employer was still obliged to pay his full rate of contribution; see Appendix II of this chapter.

This position has recently been modified; married women paying a reduced rate contribution on 6th April 1977 may continue to do so indefinitely, *provided* they remain married (or secure a widow's benefit) and do not either:

i)   opt to pay full contributions,

or ii)   take a break of more than 2 years from work after 5th April 1978.

Married women paying *full* contributions on 6th April 1977 who wish to pay at the reduced rate must have opted to do so by 11th May 1977. If they have not exercised their option by this date they will not normally be allowed to change to a reduced rate of contribution later.

Women marrying after 5th April 1977 *must* pay the full rate of contribution.

A married woman not working in April 1977, but who may resume work *before* April 1980, will be able to delay her choice, but only until April 1980. If by that date no choice has been made, the option will lapse and thereafter she will have to pay the full rate.

Self Employed

Although this book primarily deals with company executives, certain of its topics also affect the self employed Schedule D taxpayer. Therefore, a brief resumé of their national insurance and social security position is included here.

As explained earlier, the self employed Schedule D taxpayer is liable to pay a flat rate Class 2 weekly contribution *plus* an earnings related Class 4 contribution.

The present flat rate Class 2 contribution is £2.66p per week for men and £2.55p per week for women; see Appendix II. However, if the self employed earnings are anticipated to be less than £875 during the fiscal year 1977/78, the Schedule D taxpayer can apply for exemption from this Class 2 contribution.

The Class 4 contribution is fixed at a flat rate of 8% on that range of profits falling between £1,750 and £5,500 per annum. These Class 4 contributions, which are not deductible for income tax purposes, are normally collected by the Inland Revenue along with the Schedule D income tax liability.

If the contributor has two jobs simultaneously, one as an employee (Class 1) and one in self employment (Classes 2 and 4), he will be liable to pay contributions under each Class. However, if it is anticipated that the total income will exceed the upper earnings limit of £105, then either the excess contributions will be refunded, or the taxpayer may apply for a deferment of the Class 2 and Class 4 contributions until the end of the tax year. Any self employed taxpayer wishing to defer payment of contributions for the 1977/78 tax year should have applied to the DHSS by 6th April 1977.

Unless arrangements are made for payment through a bank or the National Giro, the Schedule D taxpayer must pay his Class 2 contributions each week by affixing to his contribution card national insurance stamps purchased from any post office. These stamps should be stuck on the appropriate weekly space in the card and cancelled by writing the date across them in ink. A contribution card is obtainable from the local Social Security office.

The precise contributions payable by the self employed are listed in Appendix II to this chapter. The benefits received by a self employed taxpayer in return for these contributions are modest:

i)   *Flat rate* sickness benefit.

ii) Invalidity benefit.

iii) Maternity benefit.

iv) Widow's benefit.

v)   Retirement pension (basic).

vi) Child's special allowance.

vii) Death grant.

The self employed *do not* receive unemployment benefit, and any accidents or diseases resulting from self employment do not entitle the Schedule D taxpayer to any of the industrial injuries benefits available to the Schedule E taxpayer.

Voluntary Contributions

Anyone not liable to Class 1, Class 2 or Class 4 contributions may pay *voluntary* flat rate Class 3 contributions. These voluntary payments are invariably made to secure a limited range of benefits, particularly retirement pension, for persons whose contribution record is not otherwise good enough.

The present level of Class 3 contributions is set out in Appendix II.

Payment of Class 3 contributions will give entitlement to the following benefits:

i)   Maternity Grant.

ii)   Widow's benefit.

iii)   Retirement pension.

iv)   Child's special allowance.

v)   Death grant.

Class 3 contributions must be paid within certain time limits if they are to count towards specific benefits. For example, to secure retirement pension and widow's benefits the Class 3 contribution must normally be paid before the end of the second tax year following the year to which the contributions relate (i.e. contributions for the 1976/77 fiscal year must be paid on or before 5th April 1979).

Anyone living in Great Britain may pay Class 3 contributions for any income tax year during which that person has paid insufficient Class 1 or Class 2 contributions to make that year a "reckonable year".

Overseas Aspects

Most Western countries nowadays have sophisticated social security systems, and anyone working overseas for a reasonable period of time will usually fall within the scope of that particular territory's system. Generally speaking the contributions payable in overseas territories tend to be somewhat higher than those in the UK.

1.   People Coming to Great Britain

An overseas person coming to Great Britain to work is usually liable to pay Class 1 contributions from the date when his employment in Great Britain begins. The liability is irrespective of whether he is working here for a British or a foreign employer. However, the employer is only usually liable to pay secondary employer's contributions if he has some form of presence or place of business in Great Britain.

Liability to pay Class 2 contributions (self employed) arises if the person is regarded as ordinarily resident in the UK for tax purposes. If he is not ordinarily resident, his obligation to pay Class 2 contributions is deferred until he has been resident here for at least 26 out of the previous 52 weeks. Class 4 liability is related strictly to income tax liability: that is, if a person produces taxable profits in the UK liable to UK income tax, then Class 4 contributions will be levied at 8% on the appropriate portion of the profits. If no profits arise which are liable to UK tax, there will be no Class 4 contribution.

A person is entitled to pay voluntary Class 3 contributions during any year in which he is resident in Great Britain.

2. Persons Leaving Great Britain

If an employee leaves the UK, having previously been resident here, then full Class 1 contributions (both primary and secondary) will be payable on all earnings in the UK for the first year after departure, provided that:

i) the employee remains "ordinarily resident" in Great Britain,

and ii) the employer has a place of business in Great Britain.

However, no Class 1 contributions are payable if the employee goes on an overseas payroll, or if some form of reciprocal agreement with the overseas country provides otherwise.

If the employee is no longer liable to pay Class 1 contributions, i.e. after the expiry of 52 weeks from leaving the UK, he is entitled to pay Class 3 contributions on a voluntary basis until he returns to the UK. If he returns home on paid leave, a liability to Class 1 contributions will arise if the period of his stay exceeds 26 weeks; if such a liability arises, the employee will also incur a further 52 weeks' liability when he starts working abroad again (see above).

3.   Reciprocal Agreements

The social security arrangements within the EEC provide for equality
of treatment and the protection of benefit rights for employees and
pensioners (and their dependants) moving between EEC countries,
provided they are either nationals of one of the EEC countries or
stateless persons or refugees permanently resident in the EEC. UK
nationals working for an employer in this country, and thus paying
Class 1 contributions, will therefore be covered by the EEC arrangements, as will their dependants. Leaflets SA.28 and SA.29 describe
these arrangements in detail, but it should be stressed that they are only
of benefit to Class 1 contributors; they do not apply to the self
employed (or non-employed). Apart from the EEC, other countries
have reciprocal social security agreements with the UK.

APPENDIX I

Leaflet NI.5   Industrial Injuries — Injury Benefit for accidents at work

Leaflet NI.6   Industrial Injuries — Disablement benefit and increases

Leaflet NI.10   Industrial Injuries — Industrial death benefits for widows and other dependants

Leaflet NI.11   National insurance contributions for domestic workers

Leaflet NI.12   Unemployment benefit

Leaflet NI.13   Widow's benefit

Leaflet NI.14   National insurance — Guardian's allowance

Leaflet NI.15   Retirement pension

Leaflet NI.15A   Retirement pensions for widows

Leaflet NI.15B   National insurance — Retirement benefits for married women

Leaflet NI.16   Sickness benefit

Leaflet NI.16A   National insurance — Invalidity benefit

Leaflet NI.17A   National insurance — Maternity benefits

Leaflet NI.25   Guide for masters and employers of mariners

Leaflet NI.27A	1977/78 National Insurance Guidance for people with small earnings from self employment
Leaflet NI.35	National Insurance contributions for company directors
Leaflet NI.39	National Insurance and contracts of service
Leaflet NI.40	National Insurance — contributions for employees
Leaflet NI.41	National Insurance guidance for the self employed
Leaflet NI.42	National Insurance voluntary contributions
Leaflet NI.46	National Insurance contributions for nurses and midwives
Leaflet NI.48	National Insurance — Unpaid and late paid contributions
Leaflet NI.49	National Insurance — Death grant
Leaflet NI.55	Unemployment benefit for seasonal workers
Leaflet NI.92	Earning extra pension by cancelling your retirement
Leaflet NI.93	National Insurance — Child's special allowance
Leaflet NI.95	National Insurance guidance for women whose marriage is ended by divorce or annulment
Leaflet NI.105	National Insurance — Four weekly and quarterly payments: retirement pensions, widows' benefits
Leaflet NI.114	Employers Guide: contracted out employments

Leaflet NI.132	National Insurance guidance for employers of people working abroad
Leaflet NI.177A	Pensions for women who are or were married to men aged 65 or over on 5 July 1948
Leaflet NI.184	Non-contributory retirement pensions for people over 80
Leaflet NI.192	National Insurance contributions for people employed through agencies
Leaflet NI.196	Social Security benefit rates for April 1977
Leaflet NI.205	Attendance allowance
Leaflet NI.207	Benefits paid for occupational deafness
Leaflet NI.208	National Insurance contribution rates from 6 April 1977
Leaflet NI.210	Non-contributory invalidity pension
Leaflet NI.211	Mobility allowance
Leaflet NI.212	Invalid car allowance
Leaflet NP.3	Occupational pension scheme
Leaflet NP.5	Guide for employers of civil airmen
Leaflet NP.15	Employer's guide to national insurance contributions
Leaflet NP.18	Class 4 national insurance contributions for 1977/78
Leaflet NP.30	New pensions: what you pay and how you benefit
Leaflet NP.31	New pensions for women
Leaflet FB1	Family benefits and pensions

APPENDIX II

CONTRIBUTIONS AND BENEFITS

PART A: CONTRIBUTIONS

Class 1 (Earnings Related)

The rates and earnings levels set out below apply to all earnings paid on or after 6th April 1977, even though they may have been earned before that date.

	Employee*	Employer*
All categories (except those listed below)	5.75%	10.75%
1. i) People under 16	nil	nil
ii) People earning less than the lower earnings limit of £15 a week (£65 a month)		
2. Married women and widows liable to pay at reduced rates	2%	10.75%
3. Men over 65 and women over 60 who are treated as retired for national insurance purposes	nil	10.75%

* The percentages specified in this table are payable on earnings up to the upper earnings limit of £105 a week (£455 a month, £5,460 per annum). Earnings above this level do not attract contributions.

Class 2 (Flat Rate)

Men   £2.66 per week

Women   £2.55 per week

Class 3 (Flat Rate)

Men and Women   £2.45 per week

Class 4 (Earnings Related)

Men and Women   8% of business profits between £1,750 and £5,500
                  per annum

PART B: BENEFITS

The following are some of the main social security benefits presently in
force, as listed in leaflet NI196 of April 1977. Unless otherwise indicated, all cash amounts shown are weekly rates. The full allowance will
normally only be payable if the taxpayer has paid sufficient contributions for the particular benefit.

1.   Attendance Allowance (Leaflet NI.205)

Higher rate   £12.20

Lower rate   £8.15

2.   Child Benefit (Leaflet CH.1)

First child   £1.00

Each other child   £1.50

Child Benefit Increase (Leaflet CH.11)

First or only child of single parent (paid only in addition to child benefit)	£0.50

Child Increases

i) With invalidity, retirement, widow's and non-contributory invalidity pensions and invalid care allowance:

First child	£6.45
Each other child	£5.95

ii) With maternity allowance and sickness, unemployment and industrial injury benefit:

First child	£3.05
Each other child	£2.55

3. Child's Special Allowance (Leaflet NI.93)

First or only child	£6.45
Each other child	£5.95

4. Death Grant (Leaflet NI.49)

The lump sum payable depends on the age of the deceased:

Age under 3	£9.00
Age 3 – 5 inclusive	£15.00
Age 6 – 17 inclusive	£22.50

Man 18 or over (born after 4 July 1893)	£30.00
Woman 18 or over (born after 4 July 1898)	£30.00
Man born between 5 July 1883 and 4 July 1893	£15.00
Woman born between 5 July 1888 and 4 July 1898	£15.00

5. Family Income Supplement (FIS.1)

Prescribed amount	£39.00
Increase in prescribed amount for each child after first	£4.50
Maximum payment for family with one child	£8.50
Increase for each additional child	£0.50

6. Guardian's Allowance (Leaflet NI.14)

First or only child	£6.45
Each other qualifying child	£5.95

7. Industrial Death Benefit (Leaflet NI.10)

Widow's pension: first 26 weeks	£21.40
Widow's pension: higher permanent rate	£15.85
Widow's pension: lower permanent rate	£4.59

Allowances for Children

Paid with widow's pension:	First child	£6.45
	Each other child	£5.95
Paid otherwise:	First child	£3.05
	Each other child	£2.55

8. Industrial Disablement Benefit (Leaflet NI.6)

i) PENSION

Disablement	Man or Woman	People under 18	Disablement	Man or Woman	People under 18
100%	£25.00	£15.30	50%	£12.50	£7.65
90%	£22.50	£13.77	40%	£10.00	£6.12
80%	£20.00	£12.24	30%	£7.50	£4.59
70%	£17.50	£10.71	20%	£5.00	£3.06
60%	£15.00	£9.18			

10% or less £2.50 payable only for pneumoconiosis assessments

ii) *GRATUITY (lump sum payment)

Disablement	Gratuity	Disablement	Gratuity	Disablement	Gratuity
19%	£1660	12%	£1079	6%	£581
18%	£1577	11%	£996	5%	£498
17%	£1494	10%	£913	4%	£415
16%	£1411	9%	£830	3%	£332
15%	£1328	8%	£747	2%	£249
14%	£1245	7%	£664	1%	£166
13%	£1162				

* Period of assessment beginning on or after 17 November 1976. If assessment is for less than seven years, gratuity will be reduced proportionately.

iii) Increases paid with disablement benefit:

a) **Special Hardship Allowance**

Maximum allowance   £10.00

Overall maximum with disablement benefit   £25.00

b) **Hospital Treatment Allowance**

  Allowance will bring disablement benefit up to   £25.00

c) **Constant Attendance Allowance**

Normal maximum	£10.00
Intermediate rate	£15.00
Maximum in exceptionally severe cases	£20.00

d) **Exceptionally Severe Disablement Allowance**   £10.00

e) **Unemployability Supplement**   £15.30

  (Entitlement not affected if claimant capable
  of earning not more than £468 a year)
  Increases for dependants and age allowance
  (invalidity allowance) are paid as with
  invalidity pension.

9. Industrial Injury Benefit (Leaflet NI.5)

Man or woman	£15.65
Person under 18	£12.90
Increase for wife or adult dependant	£8.00

10. Invalid Care Allowance (Leaflet NI.212)

Man or woman (usually single)	£9.20
Increase for wife or adult dependant	£5.60

11. Invalidity Benefit (Leaflet NI.16A)

Invalidity Pension	£15.30
Increase for wife or adult dependant	£9.20

Invalidity Allowance payable in addition for incapacity beginning:

Under age 35 or before 5 July 1948	£3.20
Age 35–44	£2.00
Age 45–59 (men) or 45–54 (women)	£1.00

12.   Maternity Benefit (Leaflet NI.17A)

Maternity grant (lump sum)	£25.00
Maternity allowance	£12.90

Earnings-related supplement (see sickness/unemployment benefit, item 17 below)

13.   Mobility Allowance (Leaflet NI.211)   £5.00

14.   Non-contributory Invalidity Pension (Leaflet NI.210)

Man or single woman	£9.20
Increase for wife or adult dependant	£5.60

15.   Pneumoconiosis, Byssinosis and Miscellaneous Diseases Benefit Scheme (Leaflet PN.1)

Allowance for the totally disabled	£25.00
Allowance for the partially disabled	£9.20

16.   i) Retirement Pension (Leaflet NI.15)

Man or woman (own contributions), or widow (late husband's contributions)	£15.30
Married couple	£24.50
Married woman (husband's contributions)	£9.20
Increase for wife or adult dependant	£9.20
Increase for pensioner over 80	£0.25

.ii) **Graduated Pension (Leaflet GR.20A)**

Amount paid for every unit of £7.50 (man) or
£9 (woman) graduated contributions paid before
6 April 1975   2½p

iii) **Non-contributory Retirement Pension for People over 80
(previously known as Old Person's Pension) (Leaflet NI.184)**

Man, single woman or widow   £9.20

Married woman   £5.60

**17. i) Sickness Benefit (Leaflet NI.16) and Unemployment Benefit
(Leaflet NI.12)**

If you are claiming unemployment benefit, remember to take
your P45 tax form when you claim.

Man under 65 and single woman or widow under 60   £12.90

Married woman under 60   £9.20

Man over 65 or woman over 60 will get retirement
·pension rate

Increase for wife or adult dependant   £8.00

ii) **Earnings-related Supplement (Leaflet NI.155A)** is payable in
addition to sickness/unemployment benefit or maternity allowance, but cannot increase the benefit or allowance to more
than 85% of average weekly or reckonable weekly earnings (as
appropriate).

Maximum supplement based on average weekly
earnings of £48 or more in 1973/74 tax year.   £9.37

Maximum supplement based on average weekly
earnings of £54 or more in 1974/75 tax year.   £10.27

Maximum supplement based on reckonable weekly
earnings of £69 or more in the 1975/76 tax year.   £12.18

18.   **Supplementary Pensions and Allowances (Leaflets SB.1 or SL.8)**

If you are over pension age you may benefit from a claim if your income after paying rent is under:

£15.70 a week for a single householder (£15.95 if over 80)

£24.85 a week for a husband and wife (£25.10 if either over 80)

If you are under pension age and do not qualify for the long-term rate, you may benefit from a claim if your income after paying rent is under:

£12.70 a week for a single householder

£20.65 a week for a husband and wife

If you have children your income can be higher and you may still be eligible.

19.   **War Pensions (Leaflet MPL.151)**

100% disablement pension	£25.00
Unemployability allowance	£16.30
Widow's pension	£19.80

Officers and their widows are paid at an annual rate. Full details of rates and allowances are given in leaflet MPL.151.

20.   **Widow's Benefits (Leaflet NI.13)**

Widow's Allowance	£21.40

Widow's Earnings-related Addition. Paid in addition to widow's allowance. Calculated as for earnings-related supplement (see above) based on late husband's earnings but not subject to 85% limit.

Widowed Mother's Allowance   £15.30

Widow's Pension   £15.30

Age-related Widow's Pension. "Age" is at time of husband's death, or when widowed mother's allowance stops:

Age 40	£4.59	Age 44	£8.87	Age 48	£13.16
41	£5.66	45	£9.95	49	£14.23
42	£6.73	46	£11.02		
43	£7.80	47	£12.09		

21. Workmen's Compensation (supplementation) Scheme (Leaflet WS.1)

Basic rate inclusive of workmen's compensation   £2.00

Major incapacity allowance   £25.00

Lesser incapacity allowance (maximum rate)   £9.20

The Government has announced certain improvements in benefits, some to take effect on 14th November 1977 and others in April 1978. For example, the basic old age pension is increased to £17.50 a week for a single person and £28 for a married couple as from 14th November 1977. The child benefit is to be increased from April 1978 such that for every qualifying child a payment of £2.30 a week is made, with no distinction between the first and subsequent children, and the supplement to one-parent families is to be increased to £1.

CHAPTER 12

SELF EMPLOYMENT — IS THIS A BETTER ALTERNATIVE?

People who work on their own account — the sole trader, the professional partner, the freelance journalist etc. — are self employed and are taxable under Schedule D on the profits or gains from their trade, profession or vocation. They also pay a different level of national insurance contributions.

A question which often arises is whether people are in a stronger financial position by being self employed. This chapter therefore seeks to itemise some of the main distinctions between self employed and employed taxpayers. Not all the items chosen for comparison relate to taxation or national insurance; some of the distinctions are of a general financial nature but which are nevertheless considered to be worthy of inclusion.

Two further points should be made:

i)   The following list of comparisons is by no means exhaustive but merely an indication of some of the more important ones. Readers may be able to add to the list from their own personal experience.

ii)   The chapter does *not* touch on the more philosophical issues such as whether employed people enjoy more security than the self employed, whether the self employed work harder than employees, whether many employees would like to become self employed but are precluded from doing so owing to lack of personal capital and so on. These are subjective issues where a wide divergence of view is possible.

Calculation of Taxation Liability

As has been seen from previous chapters in this book, employees are taxable on what may be termed an "actual" year basis. That is to say the earnings for a fiscal year are taxable in the same fiscal year.

Example

Brian Jelley, an executive of The Dessert Banking Corporation of the Middle East receives a salary of £1,000 per month plus a bonus in March 1978 of £3,000. His emoluments for the fiscal year 1977/78 are therefore £15,000 (i.e. £12,000 plus £3,000 bonus) and this will be regarded as the amount of his taxable income for that fiscal year.

Schedule D tax liability, however, is worked out on a somewhat different basis. With the exception of the opening and closing years of a business, the rule is that a Schedule D taxpayer is taxable by reference to the business profits revealed by the accounts ending in the *previous* fiscal year.

Example

Christopher Barrett is a partner in a firm of financial consultants Barrett, Stopper and Barrett. He is entitled to 50% of the firm's profits as shown by the accounts.

The firm makes up its accounts to June 30th, 1976. The profits shown by the accounts are £50,000 which means that Christopher Barrett's share is £25,000.

For the fiscal year *1977/78* (April 6th 1977 — April 5th 1978) Christopher Barrett will be taxable on an income of £25,000. Thus the profits shown up by the accounts ending in the preceding year (i.e. those ending on 30th June 1976, which is in the 1976/77 fiscal year) form the basis of the Schedule D tax assessment for the *following* tax year.

From the foregoing it will be seen that the Schedule D taxpayer has a cash flow advantage if his income is rising, because he is in effect paying tax on last year's income out of this year's profits. On the other hand, if his income is falling, he is at a disadvantage because he may well have spent the income earned in the previous year, but the tax bill relating to it will not be received until the present fiscal year when his actual income could be much reduced.

To summarise therefore, the Schedule E taxpayer pays tax on his income for the actual fiscal year and the Schedule D taxpayer normally pays tax on the profits of the business for the accounts ended in the previous fiscal year.

Collection of Tax

As was explained in Chapter 2, Schedule E taxpayers suffer income tax (at both basic and higher rates) by deduction at source by the employer under the PAYE system. He therefore pays tax on a regular weekly or monthly basis.

The Schedule D taxpayer on the other hand pays tax direct to the Inland Revenue. The tax is collected in two equal half yearly amounts, the first payment being due on 1st January in the year of assessment and the next payment being due 6 months later in July of the following tax year.

Example

A firm of solicitors make up their accounts to December 31st 1976 and reveal a profit of £15,000. This amount would be taxable in the fiscal year 1977/78. The first instalment of tax would be due on 1st January 1978 and the second instalment 6 months later in July 1978.

In some cases the Schedule D income will not have been finally assessed by the due date and, because tax cannot be levied until an assessment specifying the amount of profits or income taxable has been finalised, the actual date of tax payment may be somewhat later than shown above. The Inland Revenue has recently introduced rules charging interest on late payment of income tax, designed to discourage accounts being presented late and payment of tax being made late. The present interest rate is 9% and any interest so charged is not deductible for tax purposes.

From the above it will be seen that the self employed taxpayer enjoys a greater cash flow advantage in payment of tax than his Schedule E colleague.

Expenses Deductible in Computing Tax Liability

For an expense to be deductible for Schedule E tax purposes, that expense must be said to have been properly incurred "wholly, exclusively *and necessarily*" in the performance of the duties of the office or employment. Chapter 2 explained how difficult it can be to obtain expense relief under Schedule E. The real problem is the word "necessarily" because, while it may be a relatively simple task to prove that an expense has been "wholly and exclusively" incurred, the requirement to be "necessarily" incurred severely limits expense relief.

The Schedule D taxpayer, however, is entitled to deduct all expenses described as merely "wholly and exclusively" expended for the trade, profession or vocation. The requirement to prove that an expense is "necessarily" incurred is not present and in practical terms this means that expense claims made by the Schedule D taxpayer are far easier to prove than those made by the Schedule E taxpayer.

As an illustration, at the time of writing this book certain problems were being experienced by divers operating on the North Sea oil and gas fields. Hitherto they had been regarded as Schedule D taxpayers and in consequence were free to deduct the cost of hotel accommodation, telephone calls and similar payments in computing their tax liability. The Inland Revenue, however, has recently contended that in reality they have a contract of service (as explained in detail in Chapter 2) and in consequence they should be taxable under the provisions of Schedule E. This has led to a number of divers leaving the North Sea to work overseas because a reclassification of their taxation status from Schedule D to Schedule E would cost them too much.

Pension Provision

Chapter 10 of this book dealt in some depth with the topic of private pension arrangements.

The Schedule E taxpayer can be entitled to substantial benefits on a tax free basis. He may receive a pension of up to two-thirds of final salary, he may provide death in service life assurance cover of up to four times current salary for his dependants free of capital transfer tax and he may take up to one and a half times his final salary as a tax free gratuity on retirement. It is possible for *all* the costs of such pension and life assurance arrangements to be met by the employer without these costs ranking as a taxable benefit in kind on the Schedule E taxpayer concerned. This is so even though the payments may relate to executives subject to the more penal benefit in kind rules introduced by the Finance Act 1976.

The Schedule D taxpayer on the other hand is not able to secure such advantageous benefits. Whereas no limit is imposed on employer sponsored pension schemes, the self employed taxpayer is restricted in the amount of tax deductible contributions he may pay over each year to secure a pension. Except for older taxpayers, the limit is £3,000 or 15% of the "net relevant earnings" (defined in Chapter 10). Furthermore any life assurance benefit secured as part of an overall self employed pension scheme is potentially subject to capital transfer tax. Obviously the self employed has to pay all the contributions himself and cannot benefit from any employer's additional payment.

Readers wishing to pursue this subject in more detail should perhaps re-read Chapter 10 but the basic message is that the Schedule D taxpayer is substantially worse off in terms of tax reliefs relating to pension entitlements than the Schedule E taxpayer.

Necessity to Provide Accounts

The Schedule E taxpayer completes a tax return each year and from this the Revenue prepare a notice of coding. The employer is advised of this notice of coding and he is then responsible for deducting tax each pay day by reference to the code number allocated to the particular employee and he then accounts for such tax deduction direct to the Inland Revenue. Nothing further is required from the employee who will receive advice as to his pay, national insurance contributions and tax deduction each pay day and will receive at the end of the fiscal year a summary of his gross pay and gross deductions for that year.

The Schedule D taxpayer on the other hand has to account for income tax on the income or profits of his particular trade, profession or vocation. This involves the maintenance of proper books of account and, almost invariably, the production of a profit and loss account showing the results of the trading for the business year. These accounts — usually prepared by a firm of accountants — are then submitted to the Inland Revenue for scrutiny and, when the accounts have been agreed, income tax is charged accordingly.

On the 15th October 1976, Sir William Pile (Chairman of the Board of Inland Revenue) stated that the Inland Revenue was about to adopt a more discriminating approach to the way they enquire into the accuracy of business accounts and the tax computations which depend on them. In this statement it was made clear that the impact of the new approach would be felt mainly by the small taxpayer. In essence the Revenue are going to be substantially more selective in the enquiries they make. This will mean that they will not raise points on the vast majority of Schedule D accounts submitted to them but will concentrate on particular returns and will investigate *much more thoroughly* those accounts selected for examination. This system has now commenced.

VAT

Emoluments taxable under Schedule E should be free of VAT liability.

Schedule D taxpayers, however, engaged in a trade, profession or vocation will (unless their *turnover* — not "profits" — is below the threshold limit) have to account for VAT in the ordinary way. The increased paperwork resulting from the obligation to collect tax on the Government's behalf (and account for it to Customs and Excise) is proving a substantial burden to many Schedule D taxpayers.

Social Security

This subject was covered in Chapter 11, to which reference should be made.

The Schedule E taxpayer will pay Class 1 contributions (as will his employer). At present, the level of employees' primary Class 1 contributions is 5.75% of earnings up to a maximum limit of £105 a week (or the appropriate monthly equivalent). In return for this payment the employee is entitled to all social security benefits generally available.

The self employed Schedule D taxpayer on the other hand now pays Class 2 contributions (at a flat rate per week) plus Class 4 contributions equal to 8% of profits falling in the range £1,750 – £5,500. The introduction of Class 4 contributions (which are not deductible for income tax purposes) does not increase the Schedule D taxpayer's entitlement to social security benefits.

The self employed do rather badly out of the social security system and their contributions only entitle them to a rather limited range of benefits. For example:

a)   They are not entitled to any form of unemployment pay.

b)   Whereas Schedule E Class 1 contributors going overseas to the EEC are covered by reciprocal arrangements made with the UK, the Schedule D Class 2/4 contributor is not covered and thus is well advised to make his own private arrangements for adequate health and medical insurance.

Legal Aspects

It would be quite impossible to cover all the legal distinctions between Schedule E and Schedule D taxpayers but the following two distinctions may be considered as illustrations of some of the factors to bear in mind:

1.   In recent years there has been much legislation dealing with employment protection. The range includes the right to belong to a trade union, actions for wrongful dismissal, equality of opportunity irrespective of sex and race, redundancy provisions and security of occupation to pregnant women. None of this protection is available to the Schedule D taxpayer.

2.   The employer (possibly the Schedule D taxpayer) will usually be liable for all wrongful acts committed by the Schedule E employee in the course of that employee's duties. Thus in practical terms the employee is not usually exposed to a risk of legal action.

The Schedule D taxpayer on the other hand runs all the legal risks associated with business dealings. For example, in the case of partnerships, the partners carry a joint and several liability for the acts of the other partners committed in the course of the business. Also, if one of the partners does not meet his personal income tax, the other partners may have to pay the debt due even at the risk of personal bankruptcy.

SUMMARY OF SOURCES

There are a number of sources from which information has been obtained for this book.

These are set out below together with the abbreviation, if any, used in the text.

National Insurance Act 1911
National Insurance Act 1946
Finance Act 1956
Income and Corporation Taxes Act 1970 (T.A.1970)
Finance Act 1970 (F.A.1970)
Finance Act 1971 (F.A.1971)
Finance Act 1972 (F.A.1972)
Finance Act 1974 (F.A.1974)
Finance No. 2 Act 1975 (F.A. (No. 2) 1975)
Social Security Pensions Act 1975
Finance Act 1976 (F.A.1976)
Finance Act 1977 (F.A.1977)

INDEX